AF505217

I would like to dedicate this book to almighty first.

Next, I would like to dedicate this book to my friends and family.

Last but not least, I dedicate this book to my colleagues and research guide, who guided me in every point of my research work.

A RESEARCH NOTE WIRELESS SENSOR NETWORKS - CLUSTERING APPROACH

KALAI KANNAN PACKIRISAMY & DR. VIDHYA S

Copyright © Kalai Kannan Packirisamy & Dr. Vidhya S
All Rights Reserved.

This book has been published with all efforts taken to make the material error-free after the consent of the author. However, the author and the publisher do not assume and hereby disclaim any liability to any party for any loss, damage, or disruption caused by errors or omissions, whether such errors or omissions result from negligence, accident, or any other cause.

While every effort has been made to avoid any mistake or omission, this publication is being sold on the condition and understanding that neither the author nor the publishers or printers would be liable in any manner to any person by reason of any mistake or omission in this publication or for any action taken or omitted to be taken or advice rendered or accepted on the basis of this work. For any defect in printing or binding the publishers will be liable only to replace the defective copy by another copy of this work then available.

Contents

Foreword

This book is not just a book but an must study guide for the researchers aiming at gaining a reasonable knowledge in the Wireless sensor networks domain. I recommend this book strongly for the researchers and academicians to go through the various review notes presented effectively. I appreciate the authors effort in writing this book for researchers and sure that it will act as guiding manual for all the researchers and academic experts interested in this WSN domain.

Mr. A.P. Christopher Arokiaraj

Preface

Its my pleasure to present this book to the researchers interested in doing research on wireless sensor networks.I hope the content of the book would really impress the researchers and academicians concentrating on the Wireless sensor network domain.

Wireless sensor networks has reached a substantial growth in the field of advanced networks with the future technologies like IoT, AI and ML.Here in this research review note I had covered a lot of content related to increasing the lifetime of the wireless sensor networks.

Two important areas like clustering and routing were playing a major role in increasing the lifetime of the wirless sensor networks.The review notes would cover the hierarchial flow of various protocols, its merits and demerits with the aspect of various clustering and routing algorithms and protocols.

Acknowledgements

I'm extremely grateful to the authors and all the researchers for their support and motivation in writing this wonderfull book on Wireless sensor networks. I'd like to express my deepest thanks to my research guide for her valuable effort and moral support in drafting the content for this book. I would like to extend my deepest gratitude to my friends for their constant encouragement and support in making this book. I would like to pay my special regards to my colleagues for their technical hints and support for every concepts of this book.

Prologue

This book comes with four important chapters all with Introduction, Data collection methodology, Algorithms and protocols used, Simulation process, results and Discussions and various references.

Chapter 1 Focuses on various parameters involved in increasing the lifetime of the WSN. Among these parameters the clustering process and routing techniques pays much attention for increasing the survival time of the entire network.

Chapter 2 Imbibes on the Clustering strategies used for increasing the network lifetime with various LEACH protocol versions and their working process with results.

Chapter 3 Insists on the Clustering protocol based on various traditional approach followed with tables and discussions.

Chapter 4 Discusses on the role of Fuzzy based technique that influences the clustering protocol in selecting the cluster head among various motes present in the clusters of the WSN.

Above all these contents concentrates on the survival time of the motes in the WSN with the aspects of clustering with Cluster head selection and along with routing of the data between the sensors to the base station of the WSN.

CHAPTER ONE

Parameters Influence in Increasing the Lifetime of the Wireless Sensor Networks

INTRODUCTION

Wireless sensor networks with various parameters that influence the lifetime have fascinated the researchers to focus on the increasing its lifetime. Due to their large scope of implementation in various fields which leads to maintenance of the lifetime with various constraints. Here in this chapter survey is been done in order to increase the lifetime of the nodes of WSN by concentrating on various stringent parameters. Though the energy management schemes directly influence the lifetime of the WSN, here we are focusing on various algorithms or protocol and the methodology or approach followed with list of parameter remarks which gives the complete information about various parameters which influence the WSN. The parameters include node management, energy balancing, MAC layer, routing policies, transmission policy, device management, load balancing, duty cycling, mobile sink based, cross layer optimization.

Terminologies: Node management, Energy balancing, Routing Policy, Transmission Policy, Extending Lifetime.

OVERVIEW

Recently the technological advancement in various WSNs applications like IOTs, cloud computing, military, environment, health, entertainment, transportation, crisis management, smart spaces, and disaster prevention leads to create a great interests among the academicians, researchers, manufacturers and their clients. Normally WSN is a spatially arranged autonomous sensor nodes used in many applications like defence, industry monitoring and health monitoring for measuring various environmental and physical conditions like pressure, temperature etc. With the usage of IOT based applications the implementation of WSN dramatically increases and this is the technology which changes the technological influence of the whole world with a different picture. These WSN works autonomously and these sensors use the radio connection and use the routing strategy. Generally WSN are equipped with batteries that too recharged or changed due to various environmental conditions and also not applicable for all the cases. Here the lifetime of the sensors influenced by different parameters especially battery energy and the need for the sensors to work for a long time. The energy used by the sensor nodes must be controlled with different parameters in order to use the less power from the battery according to the application it's been implemented. However these parameters which influence in providing the maximum network lifetime and high quality of service. Increasing the lifetime is one of the main issue in managing the WSN. Though there are various energy harvesting and management schemes it is very important for the researcher to concentrate on these various parameters which influence in increasing the lifetime of the networks.

DATA COLLECTION PROCESS

Here a set of chapter is been taken which deals specifically with increasing in the lifetime of the sensor networks. Therefore which gives the detailed picture and reports of various researchers who involved in the research process of lifetime of the WSNs and effort has been taken to choose the articles and research chapters for articulating this review. The SCI indexed, Web of Science and Scopus databases has been taken to shortlist the research chapters with good citation that provides in depth research view. This review chapters analyzes the content of 25 research articles which has been published on the title of lifetime of WSN from 2002 to 2021 within different research scopes. This was organized this review into 4 stages:

1. Collection of research chapters which includes search by keywords, assortment of various research databases.
2. Selection of chapters on the basis of citation index, publisher's database like Web of Science or Scopus and focusing on the research area which deals with lifetime of the WSNs.
3. Primary analysis with detailed investigation to deliver reviewers with brief insight on the domains of the selected chapters.
4. Examination of the content of the review chapters, proposing a peculiar framework and finding of research scopes and gaps.

Parameters Influenced in Lifetime of the WSN Nodes are:

A) Battery powered nodes

- Node control algorithms
- Energy control algorithms

B) Transmission

- MAC algorithms
- Routing algorithms
- Transmission algorithms

C) System
D) Device control algorithms

Analysis of Extending the Lifetime of WSN

Generally a wireless sensor networks consists of aggregation of sensor nodes to sense and collect data pertain to the area or environment it's been implemented where these mote consists of four important parts, battery power, sensing module, data aggregation, processing and communication modules. The usage of energy is seems to be low for sensing and data processing. Most important thing is the communication module which consumes most of the energy which leads to depletion of its battery resources and in turn which decrease the lifetime of the entire networks forcibly.

Battery Controlling Techniques

Battery which plays a vital role in extending the lifetime of wireless sensor networks while designing the battery driven devices, the importance is given to its internal attributes. These internal attributes explore the internal characteristics of battery to get their charge to increase the load of power supply to the sensor nodes. Here we explain various battery controlling techniques that which improve the lifetime of WSN, various better optimizing techniques been described here with remarkable discussions.

Node Power

In 2016 S.S. Desai et al. proposed a layer based, self organizing algorithm for node power controlling application called as Distributed algorithm for node energy system (DANES), the important functionality of distributed algorithm is to preserve the lifetime and providing the network lifetime based on the strength of the node. Based on the "live" status of mote and determine whether to give instructions for waking it up or put it to sleep in the locally implemented WSN environment.

Balancing of Energy

In 2016 J. Buwaya *et al.,*, presented a general method for balancing energy among the Sensor nodes in WSNs by giving solutions using a linear modular Subgames algorithms , the centralized optimal computation(Centopt), this subgames algorithm been implemented on the modular energy balanced WSN for routing(Mod BalGames),the social optimum(Centcalopt) and the subgames algorithm been used on the classical routing game(ModCalGames), and these two algorithms with a distributed structure and distributed standard perform in a better way for experimental testing which shows improvement in the balancing energy and increase the energy efficiency and is network lifetime. In 2017 W.Wei *et al.,* presented algorithm which controls the coverage and balancing energy based on the mote positive for the WSN network model. The developed algorithm named K degree coverage algorithm which optimizes the network resources by scheduling the proper routines between the working nodes and neighboring nodes with minimal power usage leads to not only increase the coverage area of the network but also minimize the usage of power that automatically leads to increase in the lifetime of network. In 2017 W. Zhang *et al* , developed a general multi-ring probability switching (Prosuit) optimization routing model that focuses on parameter like consuming energy to transmit the information, rate of data transmission, wireless energy harvesting and also analyzing the parameters like density of the node, depth of the ring and inner ring transmitting probability which achieve increase in network lifetime. In 2018 S.P. Tirani et al , developed two energy balancing algorithms EHDT & ECDA(Energy aware high level data aggregation and CS-based data aggregation) which focusing on data collection models to increase the lifetime of network and also provides energy balancing between various nodes.

Transmission Controlling Techniques

MAC Layer Controlling Techniques

Generally, MAC layer controlling techniques are implemented MAC protocols to increase the lifetime and energy in the network efficiently. For the WSN communication the MAC protocol seems to be the bottom most protocol. The researchers are focusing on the various areas of application of WSN using various forms of MAC protocols. The MAC protocol which is based on the contention is enabled with smart nodes which use the radio link for transmitting the data by competition. One of the important and most widely used IEEE 802.11 is a MAC protocol runs based on competition which uses techniques like CSMA with CA(carrier sense multiple access with collision avoidance).The other form of MAC layer protocol are TDMA based non-collision based.

In 2004 van Hoeselt *et al.*, constructed a TDMA based E-MAC protocol which seems to be fully distributed energy- efficient, and self organized for WSNs, where a control message is passes throughout the WSNs and by making a structure of independent nodes listening to the channel randomly and selecting particular time slot which is collision free. This EMAC increases the network lifetime significantly, where the structure of the WSN is variable.

In 2017 O.Bouachir et al presented (EAMP-AIDC) Energy aware MAC protocol with adaptive individual duty cycle which is based on focusing on parameters like residual node energy application and requirements of data which optimize the active and sleep periods called as individual duty cycle. This protocol minimizes the overall usage of the power by minimizing the active period and increasing the sleep period for every mote in the WSNs.

In 2018 K.F. Ramadan et al , presented a power based MAC protocol for a node, with specific adaptive time slot which listens to the channel and solving the problem of improper allocation of power among nodes in the (ML - MAC) multilayer protocol and S-MAC protocol. The results show that the developed MAC protocol increases the fair power usage. The researcher suggesting more number of MAC protocols, but most of the techniques have disadvantage of unbalanced power usage among different motes , which leads to fast demise of low-medium energy nodes. The developed MAC protocol gives the sleep time upto 92.5% and saves 23.1% power devoted by ML-MAC & 73% power devoted by S-MAC protocol respectively.

Routing Policies for Increasing the Lifetime of WSNs

In WSNs, the important aim of routing protocols are to have a proper link between source nodes and sink nodes by not compromising some important performance characteristics like saving-energy, latency, fault tolerance and lifetime. The most important construction principle of routing protocol is concentrates on power saving that automatically leads to increases in lifetime of network.

In 2014 Z.aliouat *et al.,* developed three different clustering based routing protocols for WSNs, First protocol named (EEADC) Efficient energy aware distributed clustering routing protocol which gives a balance CHs in the distribution of the network. The second protocol named(FEEADC)- Fixed efficient energy aware distributed clustering protocol which gives a prominent addition in EEADC that gives the solution for CHs based on grid and achieves an effective CHs distributed in the WSNs. The third protocol named as (M-FEEADC) Multi-hop fixed efficient-energy aware distributed clustering uses data aggregation techniques and sleep-wake up between inter cluster multi-hop.

The important advantage of this cluster fixing which gives a balanced distribution of CHs and preserve energy by allowing every sensor node by placing far away from the Base station. The result shows an important increase in ratio in terms of network lifetime, power utilization among mostly used protocols like TEEN and LEACH protocols.

In 2017 K.A.Darabkh *et al.*, developed a protocol named as (EA-CRP) a unique energy aware and layering based clustering and routing protocol for collection of data in WSNs. It utilizes an effective multiple layered architecture to reach the goal of minimizing the power used between all the nodes that leads to efficient performance according with energy efficiency, scalability and lifetime of network.

In 2017 S. Sasirekha *et al.*, constructed an algorithm called as cluster chain mobile agent routing (CCMAR) by combining two effective algorithms called as chain-based hierarchical power efficient gathering in sensor information systems (PEGASIS) network and cluster based hierarchical LEACH routing, which constructs few clusters in the WSN and enters in to two stages to make full use of both LEACH and PEGASIS. The result shows that the developed CCMAR gives better performance besides the LEACH and PEGASIS in terms of communication delay, power consumption and lifetime of network.

In 2017 J.Wang *et al.*, created a routing algorithm called as Energy efficient basis on PSO routing algorithm with mobile sink (EPMS), associated with the technique called as virtual clustering for WSNs to choose CHs based on basic characteristics of mote like its position and residual energy, which can decrease the delay in delivering and consumes low energy and also increase the lifetime of the network.

In 2017 DZhang *et al.*, developed a general(UCNPD) unequal clustering on the basis of network partition and distance protocol for balancing the energy in WSNs that defines a ring environment by placing BS(Base station) at its center point. After that the entire parts based on distance from the node to BS, where the node is far away from BS. These nodes establish a path in this ring area to the BS and follow a timing strategy along with optimized clustering routing service protocol to choose CHs which balance and preserve power consumption and increase the network lifetime.

In 2018 G.P. Gupta *et al* , developed an (ICSA) improvised cuckoo search based clustering algorithm to give the solution for the NP-hard problem of balancing energy to select CHs in WSNs. This meta-heuristic clustering algorithm gives a more general function which helps CHs for its equal distribution to balance the communication load. This shows a better result on residual power, network lifetime of WSN.

In 2012 P. Lohan *et al.*, , for the first time announced a (GSSC) Geography based sleep scheduling and chain based routing algorithm, implements multi hop routing which is chain based to ignore the data which seems to be redundant one by identifying and switching off motes with similar information in WSNs. The results shows that increment in network lifetime been achieved comparing to the previous algorithm like PEGASIS and LEACH.

In 2002 R.C. Shah *et al* constructed a protocol named as EAR (Energy aware routing), which uses very low power additional optimal links to show some important gains. The results not only show the long-term connectivity but gives increase in lifetime of network of motes up to 40% comparing to DD routing policies.

In 2013 S. Chelbi *et al.,* designed a MEEDC (multi-hop energy-efficient routing protocol for Data controlling) where heterogeneous architecture been used to control data and various number of transmissions. This algorithm gives three important functions. First it selects the CH with high residual energy and distributes the energy among motes by making the CH to revolve in each cluster randomly. Second it implements (ordinary and advanced nodes) to manage the multi-hops problem. Third this algorithm gives better results on sensitive message controlling which decrease the trails of transmission and extended the network lifetime.

In 2016 G.S. Brar *et al.,* developed an energy based transmission routing protocol named as PDROP (PEGASIS – DSR and ORP), DSR – Dynamic source routing and ORP optimized routing protocol, this developed algorithm uses two techniques applied hybridization genetic algorithm and bacterial foraging optimization to identify the optimal paths. This routing protocol gives the best result for energy consumptions decrease in delay, error rate and also increase in throughput, which extends the network lifetime and also gives better QOS.

In 2013 L. Berbakov *et al.,* designed an optimal transmission policy for associative functioning sensor nodes (battery with energy harvesting system), used to transfer information to a base station which is far away for improving the throughput to certain limit. It's been developed that the energy harvesting sensor has infinite capability which gives optimal energy allotment throughout the WSNs that leads to increase in survival time of network.

In 2012 A. Silva *et al.,* developed energy controlling techniques, which has been combined to produce an energy efficient solution for sensor nodes and used in low duty-cycle WSNs applications. Here three important techniques is been combined called as Power Gating (PG), Power

Management (PM) and voltage regulator avoidance (VRA), finally it is been verified that the total energy loss is due to effect called as pulse current effect and to solve this flexible WSNs node been designed in a way that can deactivate and activate automatically by using software and the result shows that the node lifetime increased by multiple times.

In 2006 D. Mandala *et al.,* developed a mixed inter-cluster routing protocol called as Even-energy distribution protocol (EEDP) for a group of cluster –based energy information in WSNs. This algorithm implements a random allocation methodology to arrange CHS based on chain configuration to distribute the traffic loads.

That leads to stop creation of hot spot and management of energy consumption between CHs. This result shows that EEDP predominantly extends the lifetime of networks, while comparing with other existing protocols.

In 2009 F. Ishmanov *et al.,* developed a DCLB (Distribution clustering with load balancing algorithm to measure the volume of data, range of clusters and to creating CHs which efficiently assigns the space between clusters. In every process of clustering algorithm measures the load on current cluster by random allocation and unequal clustering methodology and construct clusters. This algorithm helps to place the clusters according to the network area width for optimization of energy and balancing the load. The result shows more efficient use of energy and prolonged network survival time.

In 2012 D. Wajgi *et al.,* developed a cluster for WSN using the clustering based protocol, transmission of data between out of clusters, collection of CHs. This uses some of the backup sensor nodes to manage the load between the various clusters in WSNs. whenever the cluster reaches its threshold value, the backup node replace the CHs. This results in efficient extension of network lifetime, scalability, reliability and also gives more throughputs.

In 2018 L. Guntupalli *et al.* designed a (4D DTMC) 4-dimensional discrete-time markov chain protocol gives the impairment effect on channel based on transmission of frame and the nature of duty-cycled MAC protocols which are synchronous for WSNs. The result shows that the developed protocols gives the accuracy on analytical models and prolonged time of network, throughput of node, efficient node energy and average transmission delay under high error based channel WSNs.

In 2006 Z. Yuanyuan *et al.*, developed an EECDS (Energy efficient CDS algorithm to provide a Connected Dominating Set (CDS) which uses two phase control methodology for associative re-development mechanism. The result show efficient power usage and extends the lifetime of network.

Table 1: Battery Controlling Problem

S. No.	Parameter	Algorithm	Result obtained
1.	Node Power	DANES & NEMA	Predict node and network lifetime to attain energy conservation modes like sleep, awake
2.	Balancing of Energy	ModBal Games & ModCal Games	Improves Energy Balance, Energy Efficiency and Network Lifetime
		K degree coverage (EBPCC) algorithm	Enhances the coverage quality of the network but also decreases power consumption that leads the network service life.
		ProSwit Algorithm	To achieve maximum network lifetime and ring with smaller distance to the sink node
		ECDA & EHDT	Enhances the network service life but also provides balanced energy and the load-balancing among different nodes

Battery Controlling

Table 2: Transmission Power Management Problem

S. No.	Parameter	Concept	Algorithm	Result obtained
1.	MAC Algorithm	Content-ion based	A node power-based MAC protocol	Enhances power efficiency and leads survival time of network.
		TDMA based	E-MAC	To reduce power consumption, while limiting loss data throughput loss and latency that extend the network lifetime
		Non-collision based	EAMP-AIDC	Increases Residual Energy, dynamic cycle, Network lifetime cycle, Network lifetime
2.	Routing Algorithm	Cluster based	EEADC, FEEADC and M-FEEADC	Enhancement in terms of network service life and power consumption
			EA-CRP	Excellent performs in case of network lifetime, scalability and energy efficiency
			CCMAR	Improves energy consumption, transmission delay, latency and lifetime of the network
			EPMS	Reduces the average delivery delay, consumes least energy and also prolongs network lifetime
			UCNPD	Balance and conserve the network power usage consumption, alive nodes and gives a longer effective service life

Transmission Power Management

Table 3: Device Control

Parameter	Algorithm	Result obtained
Device Management	Power Gating (PG), Voltage Regulator Avoidance (VRA) and Power Management (PM)	Strongly extended the network lifetime

Device Control

Table 4: Transmission Power Management Problem

S. No	Parameter	Concept	Algorithm	Result obtained
1.	Routing policies	Cluster based	ICSCA	Outperforms in case of network survival time, residual energy and total power consumption
		Geo-graphic routing	GSSC	Achieves significant increment in service life of network
		Energy routing	EAR	Achieves better network lifetime and long-term connectivity
			MEEDC	Reduces the number of transmissions that significantly prolongs the network lifetime
			EEOC	Prolonged Network Lifetime
2.	Trans-mission policy	Probability distribution	Jointly optimal transmission policy	Achieves throughput and network lifetime

Transmission Power Management

Table 5: Other Sources (Network Coding & Topology Control)

Parameter	Concept	Algorithm	Result obtained
1.Load Balancing	Enhanced balance compressed network coding	EEDP	Better load balance and expressively enhances the lifetime of network
		DCLB	Energy efficient and provides a longer lifetime
		Load Balancing using clustering	Prolonging the network lifetime, reliability, scalability and will provide high throughput by reducing energy consumption
		4D DTMC	Beneficial in terms of power efficiency of nodes, throughput, also average packet delay and service life
	Topology Control	EECDS	Prolongs to network lifetime and balancing energy

Network Coding and Topology Control

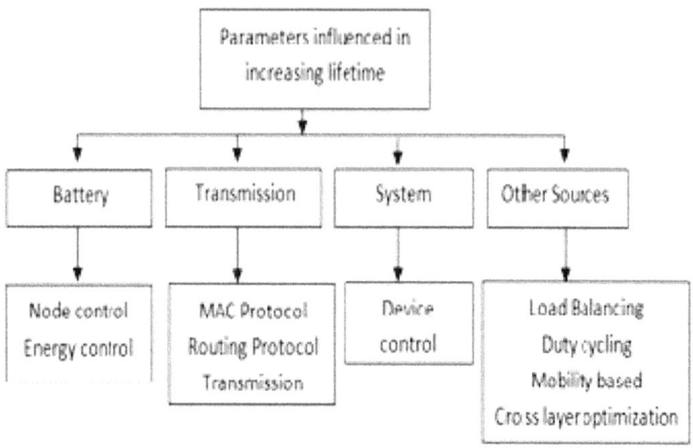

Figure 1 :Parameters for Lifetime in WSN

CONCLUSION

In the implementation and working of WSNs, the lifetime extension seems to be one of the important areas to concentrate. Here in this chapter after surveying some reputed journals and articles the aspects of extension of lifetime of WSNs were focused and discussed. We have focused on various different parameters which involve in the extension of lifetime of WSNs. There are different parameters involved like battery, transmission, System and other sources. Out of these various parameters we focused much on the first three parameters. In the first parameter Battery, We concentrated on node power and energy control and in the second parameter transmission, we concentrated on MAC protocol, routing protocol and transmission and in the third parameter, we focused on device control. Each and every parameter simulated with different algorithms and these algorithmic procedures gives the better results in increasing the lifetime of WSNs. These algorithmic results were discussed with detailed descriptions and shown with a neat table regarding the lifetime of WSNs and its extending factors.

REFERENCES

1. S.S.Desai, M.J.Nene, DANES-distributed algorithm for node energy-management for self-organizing wireless sensor networks, in: International Conference On Re-cent Trends In Electronics Information Communication Technology,IEEE,2016,pp.1296-1301. https://doi.org/10.1109/RTEICT.2016.7808041.

2. J.Buwaya, J.Rolim, Bounding distributed energy balancing schemes for WSNs via modular subgames, in: International Conference on Distributed Comput-ing in Sensor Systems (DCOSS), IEEE ComputerSociety,2016,pp.153–160. https://doi.org/10.1109/DCOSS.2016.13.

3. W.Wei,Z.Sun, H.Song, H.Wang, X. Fan, Energy balance-based steer-able arguments coverage method in WSNs, IEEE Access3536(2017)1–10 https://doi.org/10.1109/ACCESS.2017.2682845.

4. W.Zhang,Z.Zhang, H.-C.Chao, Y.Liu, P.Zhang, System-level energy balance for maximizing network lifetime in WSNs, IEEE Access 5 (2017) 20046–20057 https://doi.org/10.1109/ACCESS.2017.2759093.

5. S. PakdamanTirani, A. Avokh, On the performance of sink placement in WSNs considering energy-balanced compressive sensing based data aggregation, J.Netw.Comput.Appl.107(2018)38–55. https://doi.org/10.1016/j.jnca.2018.01.012

6. L.F.W.VanHoeselt, T.Niebergt H.J.Kipt ,P.J.M.Havingar, Advantagesof aTDMA based, energy-efficient, self- organizing MAC protocol for WSNs, IEEE (2004)1598–1602.

7. O.Bouachir, A.BenMnaouer, F.Touati, D.Crescini, EAMP-AIDC-Energy-aware mac protocol with adaptive individual duty cycle for EH-WSN, in: International Wireless Communications and Mobile Computing Conference,(IWCMC),IEEE,2017,pp.2021–2028. https://doi.org/10.1109/IWCMC.2017.7986594.

8. K.F.Ramadan, M.I.Dessouky, M.Abd-Elnaby, F.E.AbdEl-Samie, Node-pow-er-based MAC protocol with adaptive listening period for wireless sensor networks, in: AEU - International Journal of Electronics and Communications,84,Elsevier,2018,pp.46-56. https://doi.org/https://doi.org/10.1016/j.aeue.2017.10.034.

9. Z. Aliouat, S. Harous, Energy efficient clustering for wirelesssensor networks, in: International Journal of Pervasive Com-putingand Communications, 10, Emerald, 2014,pp.469–480. https://doi.org/http://dx.doi.org/10.1108/VINE-10-2013-0063.

10. K.A.Darabkh, N.J.Al-Maaitah, I.F.Jafar, A.F.Khalifeh, EACRP:a novel energy-aware clustering and routing protocol in wireless sensor networks, Comput. Electr. Eng. 72 (2018), 702–718. https://doi.org/10.1016/j.compeleceng.2017.11.017.

11. S.Sasirekha, S.Swamynathan, Cluster chain mobile agent routing algorithm for efficient data aggregation in wireless sensor network, in: Journal of Communications and Networks, 19, KICS, 2017, pp.392–401.

12. J. Wang, Y. Cao, B. Li, H. Kim, S. Lee, Particle swarm optimization based clustering algorithm with mobile sink for WSNs ,in:Future Generation Computer Systems, 76, Elsevier, 2017, pp.452–457. https://doi.org/10.1016/j.future.2016.08.004.

13. D. gan Zhang, S. Liu, T. Zhang, Z. Liang, Novel unequal clustering routing protocol considering energy balancing based on network partition & distance for mobile education, in: Journal of Network and ComputerApplications,88,Elsevier,2017,pp.1–9. https://doi.org/10.1016/j.jnca.2017.03.025.

14. G.P.Gupta,Improved cuckoo search based clustering protocol for wireless sensor networks, in: 6Th International Conference on Smart Computing and Communications, ICSCC, ComputerScience,125, Elsevier,2018,pp.234–240.

15. P. Lohan, R. Chauhan, Geography-informed sleep scheduled and chaining based energy efficient data routing in WSN, in: IEEE Students' Conference on Electri-cal, Electronics and Computer Science : Innovation for Humanity, (SCEECS), IEEE, 2012 ,pp.3–6. https://doi.org/10.1109/SCEECS.2012.6184802.

16. R.C.Shah, J.M.Rabaey, Energy aware routing for low energy adhocsensor networks, in: ProcofIEEE WirelessCommunication, 2002, pp.350–355.

17. S. Chelbi, M. Abdouli, R. Bouaziz, C. Duvallet, Multi-hop energy efficient routing protocol based on data controlling for wireless sensor networks, in: ACS Interna-tional Conference on Computer Systems and Applications (AICCSA), IEEE, 2013, pp.1–6. https://doi.org/10.1109/AICCSA.2013.6616503.

18. G.S.Brar, S.Rani, V.Chopra, R.Malhotra, H.Song, S.H.Ahmed, Energyefficient direction-based PDORP routing protocol for WSN, I EEEAccess4(2016)3182–3194 https://doi.org/10.1109/ACCESS.2016.2576475.

19. L. Berbakov, C. Antón-Haro, J. Matamoros, Optimal transmission policy for cooperative transmission with energy harvesting and battery operated sensor nodes, in:Signal Processing, 93, Elsevier, 2013,pp.3159–3170.https://doi.org/10.1016/j.sigpro.2013.04.009.

20. A.Silva,M.Liu, M.Moghaddam, Power-management techniques for wireless sensor networks and similar low-power communication devices based on non rechargeable batteries, J.Comput.Netw.Commun.(2012)1–10.https://doi.org/10.1155/2012/757291.

21. D. Mandala, F. Dai, X. Du, C. You, Load balance and energy efficient data gathering in wireless sensor networks,in: International Confer-enceon MobileAdHoc and Sensor Sysetems, IEEE,2006,pp.586–591. https://doi.org/10.1109/MOBHOC.2006.278616.

22. F.Ishmanov , S.W.Kim, Distributed clustering algorithm with load balancing in wireless sensor network, in: World Congress on Computer Science and Information Engineering (WRI), IEEE Computer Society, 2009, pp. 19 – 23. https://doi.org/10.1109/CSIE.2009.816.

23. D. Wajgi, D.N.V. Thakur, Load balancing based approach to improve lifetime of wireless sensor network, Int.J.Wirel.MobileNetw.(IJWMN)4(2012)155–167.

24. L. Guntupalli, J. Martinez-Bauset, F.Y. Li, Performance of frame transmis-sions ande vent-triggered sleep inginduty-cycledWSNs with error-prone wirelesslinks, in:ComputerNetworks, 134, Elsevier, 2018, pp.215–227. https://doi.org/10.1016/j.comnet.2018.01.047.

25. Z.Yuanyuan, J. Xiaohua, H.Yanxiang, Energy efficient distributed connected dominating sets construction in wireless sensor networks, in: ACM Proceedings of the2006 International Conference on Wireless Communications and Mobile Computing,2006,pp.797–802.

26. Jaspreet Singh, Ranjit Kaur, Damanpreet Singh, A survey and taxonomy on energy management schemes in WSN, in: Journal of systems Architecture , Elsevier, 2020.

27. Poornimha. J, A. V. Senthil Kumar and H. Mohammed Ali Abdullah, "A New Approach to Improve Energy Consumption Time and Life Time using Energy Based Routing in WSN," 2021 Emerging Trends in Industry

4.0 (ETI 4.0), 2021, pp. 1-6, doi: 10.1109/ETI4.051663.2021.9619412.

CHAPTER TWO

Clustering in LEACH protocol for increasing the lifetime of WSN

Introduction

Clustering technique is one of the most important procedures followed in the management of WSN. Now a day's various applications like factory monitoring, agriculture and health care depends on the techniques implemented in WSN. these sensor networks has its own various advantage like easy deployment, cost effective , multi functions and auto processing and follow the routine nature of routing protocols. Though there are various advantages, there are some drawbacks that yet to be focused and rectified. Those drawbacks are micro size batteries which don't have the ability to hold the energy for long time, more energy consumption while processing and routing the data packets, shortness in the lifetime nodes of WSN where it is being deployed. This chapter proposes a new algorithm which helps to increase the lifetime of Sensor networks and effective throughputs is begin achieved and enhancement of transferring time of data by decreasing the delay time. Here we concentrated on the result obtained from the developed algorithm and compare it with the existing primary LEACH protocol along with its fixing parameters. Thus the constructed adaptive clustering shows a massive improvement in terms of survival time of the WSN.

Terminologies: Clustering, lifetime, LEACH protocol, cluster head (CH), base station (BS).

OVERVIEW

WSN is a collection of more number of minute tiny sensors established in a particular area based on the specific application .Each mote consists of information, processing, sensing and data transmissions. These motes from the networks that transmit the sensed data to the sink or Base Station (BS).In the sink the collected sensed data will be processed and calculated to provide readable results. The data transmission between the sink or BS and wireless mote is managed by various protocols. One such a cluster based energy efficient routing protocol is LEACH. Here in this protocol, the entire network area is splitted into various clusters and every cluster has selected one particular node has cluster head, which is connected with all the member nodes of the cluster and the sink, collecting data from each mote of the network and transferring the aggregated data to the sink or BS.

Being a cluster head it used to perform many functions than the remaining nodes, so it used to consume more energy faster than the other nodes, which may leads to premature death of the CH. In this research chapter, we developed a new algorithm named as CH (Cluster Head) which will be selected as cluster head in a random fashion, after the death of previous CH. So, the nodes present in the WSN cluster transmits the information even if few nodes are dead, which helps to prolong the network lifetime and performance.

This LEACH protocol implements TDMA or CDMA as a routing protocol. First process of the LEACH starts with the preparation phase and ends with the processing phase. Preparation phase deals with setup of clusters and nodes. The processing phase involves in the transmission and processing called as steady state phase. Formation of clusters and selection of cluster head happens in the setup phase. Our aim is to select the CH based on DBCH algorithm and their associations with the CH approach may increases the survival time of the network, decrease the delay time and increase the throughput rate. This research chapter structured as follows, data aggregation process , Basic LEACH protocol and its relevant review study notes, Basic LEACH simulation with Plots and graphs of existing algorithm . The simulation results of the algorithm along with discussion and illustrative figures are presented. The conclusion of the research notes is presented finally.

DATA AGGREGATION PROCESS

WSN is rapidly growing with the advancement in various technologies of IOT application. Researcher is concentrating on various different parameters which could enhance the growth and also helps to improve this technology based on the growing needs of requirements and applications. But one of the important disadvantages of wireless sensor networks is the management of its lifetime and balancing of energy which may vary with the environment implemented and application used. Therefore most of the researches work focusing on these areas to fade the drawback and improve the survival time of the networks using different algorithm and various mathematical modeling structures to solve these issues.

In 2013, Sharma Et Al developed a novel algorithm for LEACH protocol in the heterogeneous WSN network and came up with discussion and results by comparing it with LEACH protocol in homogeneous WSN, for the analysis process the selected 100 X 100 meters area to check the working of protocol and they found that 10 nodes survives till last round and holds sufficient energy than the rest of other 90 more nodes which gives the increase in network lifetime and improvement in the performance of WSN. In 2014, Naveen Et al discussed on 15 different forms of clustering in WSN protocol, which gives better results in terms of energy efficiency and survival time of network and also studied on various parameters like scalability, balancing the load and energy efficiency. In 2019, as discussed by Prasad Et al , selection of cluster head using clustering algorithm seems to be one of the important factor to achieve improved performance in WSN.They constructed an algorithm called IEE-LEACH (Improved Energy Efficient LEACH Protocol) for MANET, to extend the network lifetime and decrease the energy usage by selecting CH which poses more energy comparing to all the sensor node and very closest to the sink or BS. They have used TDMA (Time Division Multiple Access) routing protocol for the LEACH protocol simulation. They tried to improve the performance of WSN by simulating the Euclidian distance between node and BS.

In 2019, Nandi Et al , sound that one of the major reasons for shortening of lifetime occurs due to increasing in the dead nodes in the WSN cluster. They used new protocol for placing BS at an optimal place of WSN which could handle various problems related to data transmission between the node and BS, and they compared the result obtained with basic LEACH protocol associated with TDMA techniques. Basically, when the sink is placed far away from the clusters, then transferring of data between node and sink will need more energy for the node which may results in shortening of the lifetime, if the sink is placed in the center of the WSN, could results in decreasing in the packet delivery time.

In 2012, Sharma et al, make a comparative study of 3 different WSN protocols, LEACH, direct transmission protocol, EEE LEACH in terms of throughput, data transferring time, where the DTx has the minimized throughput and LEACH gives the better data transfer time.

In 2015, Sharma et al [12], developed the threshold value for the DBCH algorithm and the following equation is:

$$T(x) = P / (1 - P) * (r \bmod *1 / P) + (1 - P) * (Er / E0) \quad (1)$$

Here Er represents the residual energy of each note of the WSN for the particular round and E0 is the initial energy. Here in this algorithm, they planned to select CH on the basis of node which is closer to the BS. Improvement concentrated on 2 parameter distance and energy. Along with that they focused on the distance between the nodes to CH & CH to BS and compare it and provide the results for homogeneous WSN, where all the nodes which have the equivalent proportion of energy.

BASIC LEACH PROTOCOL

In 2004, Alippi at al suggested a low energy clustering protocol for WSN (or) LEACH protocol. LEACH is a auto clustering protocol commonly, the nodes are positioned randomly and all the nodes have the probability to become the CH and which may acts as a entry point for all the nodes in the cluster and to the sink or BS based in the (2) equation: $T(x) = ((P / (1 - P) * (r \bmod (1 / P)))) $ or 0 otherwise, $n \in G$ (2)

During the setup phase the selection of CH will occurs in each round of LEACH protocol. Each and every node will generate n number between 0.0 to 1.0, when the number is less than the threshold(T), then that particular node will be chooses as cluster head, then the CH will pass a message to all the other nodes in the cluster in the same frequency range. Then using the indicator called as RSSI (Received signal strength indicator) Y.Shatnawi et al 2019, cluster will be formed. P is the probability of a sensor mote to become a CH, r represents number of rounds G is the set of nodes that have not been chooses in the last (1/p) round. Here the cluster head will form the TDMA slots for the entire node in its cluster.

Then the steady-state phase starts for the LEACH protocol. Here the data transmission process starts and data packet transferred from node to CH and the CH collecting integrates the data and forwards it to the sink. In LEACH algorithm, most important drawback is it use to consume more energy and if the cluster head death occurs results in a problem for further data communication process.

Working nature of Adaptive Cluster Head

On analyzing the working nature of LEACH protocol, it came to know that selection of cluster head plays the vital role in increasing and enhancing the network lifetime and also data transmission. We develop an algorithm which helps to improve the survival time of the network by choosing the cluster head (CH) and adaptive cluster head (ACH) in the sensor network of the setup phase for each round. Based on the discussion of previous researches, suppose if the distance between the BS and CH is less than it gives the better lifetime. So here we choose the closest node to the BS as CH and checking for the next closest node to the BS along with its residual energy level, based on this solution, all the node in the cluster will have the chance to act as CH, and the entire cluster will extends it work for longtime. Obviously gives the enhancement in the network lifetime.

Based on this solution, if the current CH becomes dead, the entire cluster doesn't goes down; instead the next node will comes into the role of CH by replacing the dead cluster head and announces itself as CH. The above procedure repeats till the presence of last active node in the cluster.

$$T(x) = P / (1\text{-} P (r \bmod(1/P) + rand(s)*Dmin \text{ to } BS * (Er/E0) \quad (3)$$

Here the threshold is set based on two criteria, the one is distance between the sink & CH and energy efficient in determining the CH1 * ACH. According with the concept of data transfer time, we insists that the location of BS should be in the middle of the WSN as shown in Figure 1, covered with 4 clusters for efficient energy management and communication between the BS & clusters.

In the above equation, the P is probability of sensing acting as CH and rand function is used to choose the sensor node as CH in a random order, where the $(Er / E0)$ gives the value of initial energy and residual energy and the distance between BS & CH is calculated using Dmin to BS.

BASIC LEACH SIMULATION

Focusing on the main issues of WSN, We concentrated on the basic algorithm, LEACH protocol, which helps to increase the performance of entire network like transmission time, throughput, and energy and network lifetime. These are the important parameter we focused on this chapter.

Figure 2 shows the basic LEACH protocol with homogeneous network topology with an 100 x 100 m coverage area.BS is centered in the network at the point of (50 , 50) m with approximate deployment of 100 nodes randomly.

We set a limit of max. no. of rounds is 5000 & clusters as 10, and the initial energy is equal to 0.5 joules. Then we fixed the packet size of the data as 4000 bits and we set the same value for all the parameters for the developed algorithm too for a fair comparison. While analyzing the basic LEACH protocol and its simulation results, it was found that, the first death of the node was in the round 1350 and the last death of the node was in the round 2000 as shown in the Figure 3. The red colored dots are the dead nodes. Active nodes in the WSN are shown in Figure 3. The figure shows the analysis of active node of basic LEACH protocol.

PLOTS AND GRAPHS

Extending the network lifetime, seems to be a main issue in WSN . So we tried to extend the lifetime of network using the developed algorithm using the similar parameter what we used for the basic LEACH protocol. Parameter are chosen based on the previous researches using the optimal values for the purpose of simulation and calculation of results are shown. The planned CH based LEACH protocol simulated parameters are shown in Table 1.

Here in this chapter, to monitor the lifecycle of the network lifetime measurement factor is used, as a whole we focused on the last dead node in the entire network. The active nodes of the developed CH based LEACH algorithm with regards to the number of rounds is shown in the Figure 4.The last dead node was found in the round 4500, comparing with the basic LEACH with the value of 2000.Out of this, the developed MAC based LEACH protocol shows increase in the lifetime of network by 50%.

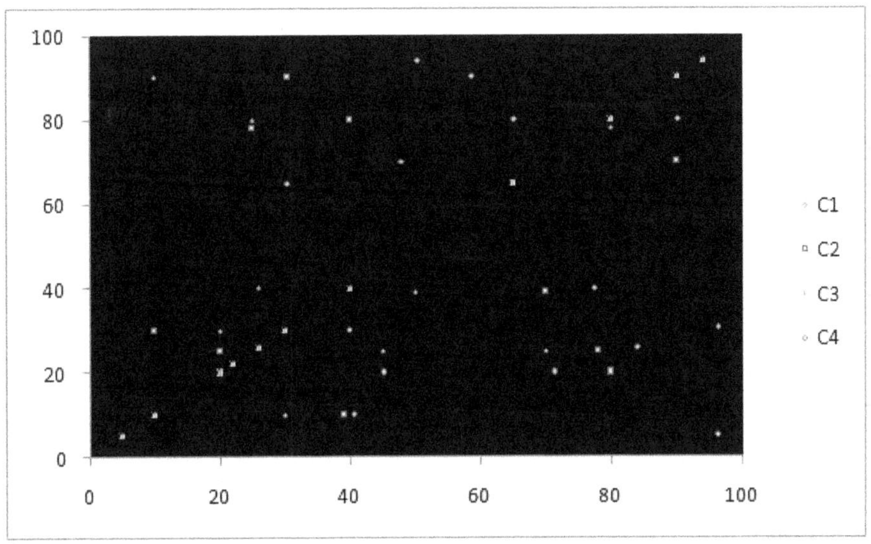

Figure 1: LEACH Protocol Topology, Rounds 2000 Dead nodes 100

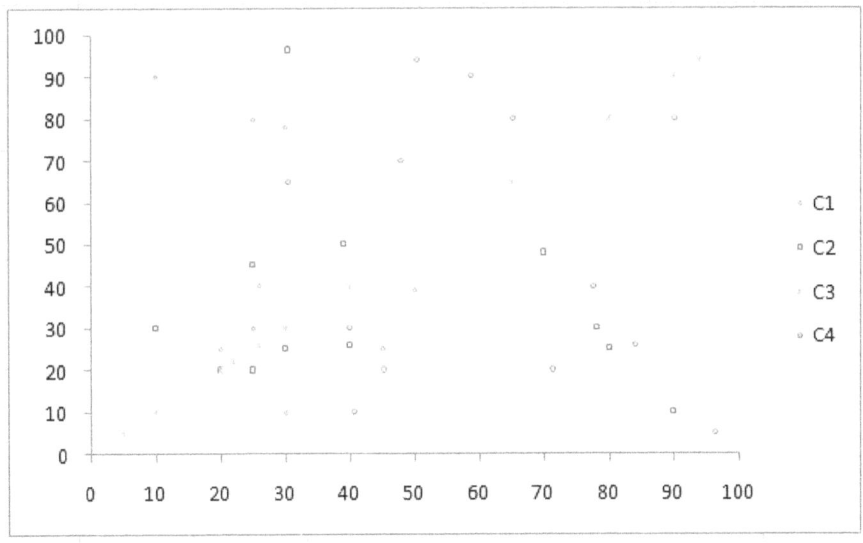

Figure 2: Picture of network during the last time, red dots denote the dead node

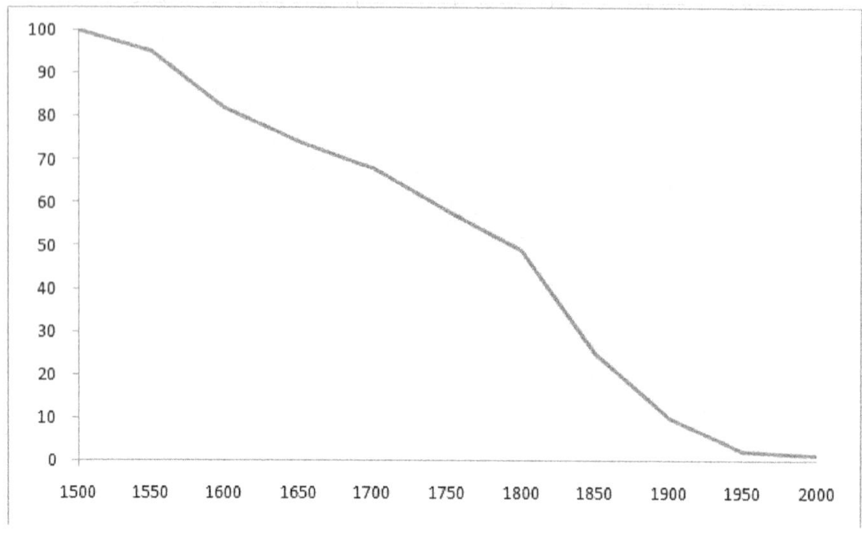

Figure 3: Active node in Basic LEACH

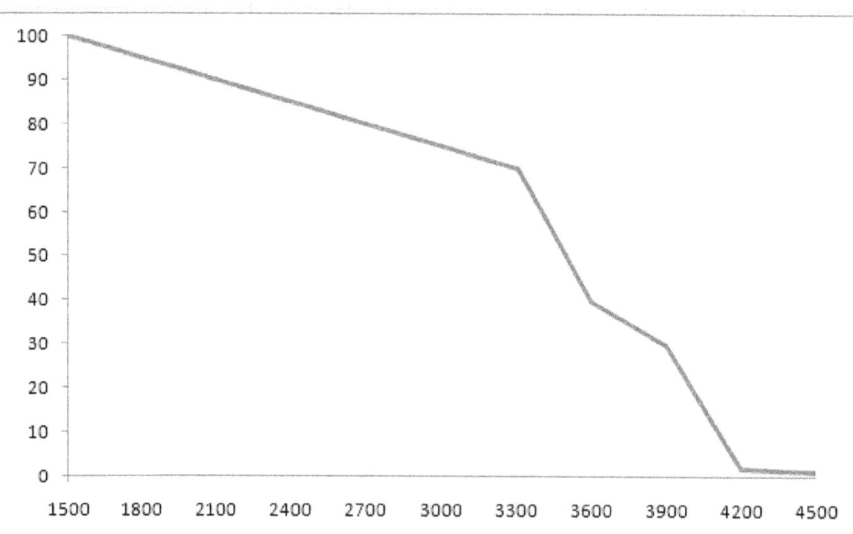

Figure 4: Active nodes ACH algorithm

Table 1 : Simulation values	
Parameter	**Value**
Sensor area	100 X 100 m
BS Point	(50, 51) m
Total node	100
Packet size	4000 bit
Control info packet size	100 bit
Initial energy	0.5 J
Probability of nodes to change to CH	0.1
Max. round	4500

Simulation Parameters

CONCLUSION

WSN are broadly implemented in different domains and applications in order to monitor and collect the data efficiently to calculate values and producing results and for taking decisions or taking appropriate action at appropriate time. Basic LEACH protocol one of the widely used protocol for the purpose of clustering and CH selection in WSN. In this chapter, we constructed a new algorithm called ACH (Adaptive cluster head, which gives the base for all the sensors to act as CH depends on the balance energy it posses. Thus results in extension of the network lifetime till the death of last node in a cluster. Therefore though some nodes become dead, the remaining sensor node in a cluster have the ability to act as CH and continuously transfer the data which automatically increase the survival tome of network. It was found that the last dead node of this algorithm was in the round of 4500 which results in the increase in the network lifetime by 50 % compared with this existing LEACH protocol also gives effective throughput during the transmission of packet between the node and CH,

CH & sink with the same network architecture setting followed with the LEACH protocol.

In future, it's possible for us to apply the ACH algorithm in different architecture and routing protocols to decrease N/W traffic and increase the lifetime along with better throughput.

REFERENCES

[1] Akyildiz, Ian F., et al. "A survey on sensor networks." IEEE Communications magazine 40.8 (2002): 102-114.

[2] M. Quwaider and S. Biswas, "Modeling energy harvesting sensors using accelerometer in body sensor networks," in Proceedings of the 8th International Conference on Body Area Networks, 2013, pp. 148–152, Accessed: Nov. 27, 2014. [Online]. Available: http://dl.acm.org/citation.cfm?id=2555348.

[3] Heinzelman, Wendi Rabiner, Anantha Chandrakasan, and Hari Balakrishnan. "Energy-efficient communication protocol for wireless microsensor networks." Proceedings of the 33rd annual Hawaii international conference on system sciences. IEEE, 2000.

[4] M. Quwaider and S. Biswas, "DTN routing in body sensor networks with dynamic postural partitioning," Ad Hoc Netw., vol. 8, no. 8, pp. 824–841, 2010.

[5] Mhatre, Vivek, and Catherine Rosenberg. "Homogeneous vs heterogeneous clustered sensor networks: a comparative study." 2004 IEEE international conference on communications (IEEE Cat. No. 04CH37577). Vol. 6. IEEE, 2004.

[6] M. Quwaider, "Real-time intruder surveillance using low-cost remote wireless sensors," in 2017 8th International Conference on Information and Communication Systems (ICICS), 2017, pp. 194–199.

[7] Sharma, Nishi, and Vandna Verma. "Energy efficient LEACH protocol for wireless sensor network." International Journal of Information and Network Security 2.4 (2013): 333.

[8] Naveen, Sharma , and Anand Nayyar. "A comprehensive review of cluster based energy efficient routing protocols for wireless sensor networks." International Journal of Application or Innovation in Engineering & Management (IJAIEM) 3.1 (2014): 441-453.

[9] Prasad, A. Y., and R. Balakrishna. "Implementation of optimal solution for network lifetime and energy consumption metrics using

improved energy efficient LEACH protocol in MANET." Telkomnika 17.4 (2019): 1758-1766.

[10] Nandi, Arnab, et al. "Centered Sink LEACH Protocol for Enhanced Performance of Wireless Sensor Network." 2019 International Conference on Automation, Computational and Technology Management (ICACTM). IEEE, 2019.

[11] Sharma, Meenakshi, and Anil Kumar Shaw. "Transmission time and throughput analysis of EEE LEACH, LEACH and direct transmission protocol: a simulation based approach." Advanced Computing 3.6 (2012): 75.

[12] Sharma, Rohini, Narendra Mishra, and Sumit Srivastava. "A proposed energy efficient distance based cluster head (DBCH) Algorithm: An Improvement over LEACH." Procedia Computer Science 57 (2015): 807-814.

[13] Alippi, Cesare, and Giovanni Vanini. "Wireless sensor networks and radio localization: a metrological analysis of the MICA2 received signal strength indicator." 29th Annual IEEE International Conference on Local Computer Networks. IEEE, 2004.

[14] Y. Shatnawi and M. Quwaider, "Congestion Control in ATM networks using PID Controller with Immune Algorithm," in 2019 10th International Conference on Information and Communication Systems (ICICS), 2019, pp. 19–24.

[15] Long-long, Xu, and Zhang Jian-jun. "Improved LEACH cluster head multi-hops algorithm in wireless sensor networks." 2010 Ninth International Symposium on Distributed Computing and Applications to Business, Engineering and Science. IEEE, 2010.

[16] Liang, Haibo, et al. "Research on routing optimization of WSNs based on improved LEACH protocol." EURASIP Journal on Wireless Communications and Networking 2019.1 (2019): 194.

[17] Comeau, Frank, and Nauman Aslam. "Analysis of LEACH energy parameters." Procedia Computer Science 5 (2011): 933-938.

[18] Chit, Tin Aye, and Khine Thin Zar. "Lifetime Improvement of Wireless Sensor Network using Residual Energy and Distance Parameters on LEACH Protocol." 2018 18th International Symposium on Communications and Information Technologies (ISCIT). IEEE, 2018.

[19] M. Quwaider and Y. Shatnawi, "Neural network model as Internet of Things congestion control using PID controller and immune-hill- climbing algorithm," Simul. Model. Pract. Theory, vol. 101, p. 102022, May 2020, doi:

10.1016 / j. simpat. 2019. 102022.

[20] Oudani, Hassan, et al. "Energy efficient in wireless sensor networks using cluster-based approach routing." International Journal of Sensors and Sensor Networks 5.5-1 (2017): 6-12.

Clustering Protocol based on traditional approach for WSN

INTRODUCTION

WSN, a broad interdisciplinary area of various major domains like computer science, engineering and mathematics researchers focusing on strengthening its performance based on various approaches and techniques. Clustering is one such an important technique with broader scope in topology management, extension of network lifetime, energy efficiency control, routing of data. Clustering is used to arrange the sensor node properly with definite structure, which helps for effective communication between the nodes and faster way of transmission of data across the networks. Maximizing the lifetime of the WSN is our objective in the scope of study, but energy dissipation and depletion that indirectly involves in extending the survival time of each nodes present in the network. Clustering techniques mainly focuses on both these areas to manage the WSN efficiently. This chapter focuses on various clustering techniques that help to increase the lifetime of WSN.

Terminologies: Clustering, network lifetime, topology management, routing protocol, base station.

OVERVIEW

WSN are mostly deployed in some remote areas for monitoring environment and measuring accurate precise information to make time based decisions. The transmission of information usually carried out by the sensor nodes present in the network. The selection of CH from a cluster and the range between the sensor nodes involves in most part of the energy consumption by the sensor node. The performance evaluation process of the WSN deals with various parameters like network lifetime, energy usage, throughput and latency. The implementation and usage of WSN are growing tremendously in different applications and its environment in the last few years. This technological growth in sensor network and its data aggregation has turned the researchers to focus on WSN. In various applications the sensor nodes as a network are used to sense and collect sensitive information which are tiny in size and embedded with battery (Garcia hernandey et al. 2007). These motes worked using wireless transmission mechanism and it communicate with one another to perform particular assigned task. The WSN were used in various major applications like health monitoring, tracking vehicles and goods, structural monitoring, biomedical, weather, fire detection, defence, industrial monitoring, etc. (Ali et al. 2019). There are numerous constraints and challenges faced by WSN, some of the issues are energy limitation, processing capabilities, communication reliability and bandwidth restrictions, etc. (Saranya and Princy et al 2012). The lifetime of the nodes are the major problem present in most of the WSN, because of the energy constraints in the battery powered sensors, the sensor may die within shorter span of time(chithaluru et al, 2019). Using various energy controlling and management techniques help the WSN to increase its performance and survival time(Rawat and chauhan 2020) .The clustering technique is one of the important method used for managing the various issues of WSN(Liu and Xuxun 2012). The clustering methodology is used for solving the problems that arises due to energy related issues and directly proportional to increase the lifetime of the network(Zeb et al, 2016).In this chapter comparison of various forms of clustering was done in order to give a clear picture about various clustering approaches used in WSN.

This concepts focuses on analysing the various clustering protocols its classification, categorization, and different parameters involved in increasing the lifetime of the WSN. The remaining part of the chapter structured as follows section II covers the literature review, in relation with clustering approaches in WSN, section III discusses on parameters influenced by clustering, section IV summarizes on two major classification of clustering protocols, Section V briefs about the criterias considered for the comparative study of clustering parameters, and Section VI deals with Conclusion of the chapter.

DATA COLLECTION PROCESS

In this review process various clustering protocol are surveyed on the basis of classification and comparison parameters. Using this survey process, one could get a clear picture of different clustering protocols used and its influence in various parameters of WSN. These protocols and its role help to solve the problems faced by the WSN.

In 2004, Al-karaki and kamal, developed a chapter which focuses on protocol functionalities & network topology. Based on the topology, the clustering protocols are categorized as flat, location-based, and hierarchy. The above protocols further categorized into QOS based, query-based, negotiation based, multi-path based. In 2005, Akkaya and younis et al , developed a chapter, the protocols are categorized into hierarchical, location-based and data-centric. Other than this, two parameters were concentrated; those are QOS and network flow process.

In 2005 Abbasi and younis , developed a chapter were based on the clustering behaviour, the protocols are focussed as constant convergence time and variable convergence time algorithm. It focuses on various areas like cluster overlapping, stability, mobility, and convergence rate and location identity. In 2008, Kumarawadu et al , review chapter concentrates on the selection of CH and its formation parameters. The protocols are categorized into biologically inspired, adjacent node information location, identity based and probability based clustering, and also various challenges faced by WSN been listed.

In 2008, Deosarkar et al , surveyed a chapter and differentiate clustering protocols as hybrid, combined, deterministic and adaptive. Further categorized the adaptive form into fixed parameters and resource probabilistic protocols that concentrate on cluster formation, CH selection, fairly positioned CHs and formation of balanced cluster.

In 2010, Boyinbode et al , the review focussed on problems faced by clustering techniques and listed a brief note on centralized, distributed and hybrid clustering. The parameters are energy, cluster size, CH arrangement, delay, hops and cluster formation.

In 2011, Li et al, categorized the clustering techniques into three forms namely, energy, load balancing and control overhead. The summary of the protocol are covered with various advantages and dis-advantages.

In 2019 Singh et al , the review was focusing on various forms of LEACH protocol its functions and performance. Two form of clustering techniques were discussed are, multihop and single hop protocols. The various parameter concentrates on scalability, energy, delay and complexity to compare the performance. In 2018, Rostami et al , the survey listed on two important forms of clustering protocols are heterogeneous and homogeneous. The various parameters are delay, network topology, CH parameter, inter cluster and intra-cluster communication, It also gives a detailed note on differentiation of various heterogeneous and homogeneous protocols. In 2019, Sharma et al , the review presents the heterogeneous forms of clustering techniques. It categorizes these heterogeneous protocols into three forms called as computational, link and energy-based. It also provides the overview & summary on CH selection, formation and determination. It provides a brief note on heterogeneity levels, disadvantages, CH parameters, etc., for comparing the protocol performance.

PARAMETERS INFLUENCED BY CLUSTERING

Though the clustering protocols are playing a major role in various different stringent parameters by its classification and categorization, there are some specific areas enhanced by clustering protocols effectively. The below statements describes on the parameters influenced by clustering technique.

Increasing network survival time

In 2017 Gherbi et al states, one of the important parameter of all the parameter is network lifetime, for calculation of the performance of WSN using clustering protocol. In 2018a Priyadarshi et al proposes that by implementing various methodologies & techniques, the energy-based protocols supports in choosing the best optimal path for data transferring process which in turn increases the network lifetime. In 2020 Rawat et al proposes that the WSN lifetime was influenced by various parameters like data communication, energy usage in transferring of data, data collection, CH selection, and deployment of nodes, increasing the performance of WSN and provides better services.

Energy Usage

In 2015 Sharma et al ; 2018b Rawat et al reviews that the energy consumption factor which involves directly in deciding the network lifetime and its extension. In 2016 Marappan et al ; 2017 yuvaraja et al ; 2020 Rajpoot et al surveys that the clustering protocol helps in decreasing the energy usage by nodes of network, in turn increase the network lifetime.

In 2019 Gupta et al ; 2020 velusamy et al; 2020 Kumaresa et al summarises that most part of the energy consumed by nodes for data communicating process in sending and receiving the data packets.

Thus the protocol helps in reducing the energy consumption of the node for packet transmission.

Scalability

In 2012 Das et al ; 2017 Naranjo et al reviews on the scalability of the WSN. The Scalability of the WSN. The scalability is one of the important parameter in evaluating the performance of WSN using clustering technique. In 2015 shokouhifar at al ; 2017 Ennajari et al ; 2018 Mazumdar et al ; 2020 Nehra et al , proposes that the clustering protocols leads to improve the network lifetime & provides the better scalability to the network.

Throughput

In 2016 yi and yang et al ; 2017 Gherbi et al ; 2018 Rostami et al reviews that the throughput is one of the major parameter in measuring the lifetime of the WSN. The increases in throughput results in better performance of the network, Delay is the total time extended in data communication process than the required time for packet delivery process. Some of the clustering technique helps in improvement of the network lifetime by minimizes the delay and increasing the throughput of the data packets to the destination node.

Coverage

In 2005 Huang & Tseng et al , Survey that the area of the environment deployed by the nodes should covered properly. The environment should be covered completely by the existing minimum nodes to collect the data from the network. Every area should be covered at least by our sensor. The clustering protocol helps in extend the range of coverage of each node which leads to complete coverage and increases in the survival time of the network. Coverage classified into point-based, area –based, barrier-based.

Load Balancing

In 2017 Sari et al , surveys that the work load of the entire network must be segregated properly between different clusters of the networks these leads to decrease the energy consumption of each node and each clusters. Thus clustering protocol helps to balance the energy usage between the nodes and clusters. Load balancing is one of the important factors which helps to increases the network survival time and also improve the performance of the WSN.

TWO MAJOR CLASSIFICATION OF CLUSTERING PROTOCOLS

Based on the functionality to give a summary on their operations and performance, the clustering protocols are, categorized into two major types: traditional clustering protocols, fuzzy-logic based clustering protocols.

Traditional clustering approach: Here in this approach, the several probability based concepts are used for clustering functions and it won't use any particular concepts for the formation of cluster, CH selection and data transferring process. In this traditional approach, basic process of clustering will be followed for CH selection & cluster formation.

Fuzzy logic based clustering technique: In 2019 Hamzah et al , to handle the unpredictability involved in the generic clustering activities such as CH selection and cluster formation the fuzzy-logic-based clustering technique. Was used .In 2013 Singh et al , surveys a model with a fuzzifier, defuzzifier and inference system based rules which could handle the constitutive unpredictability involved in the WSN by taking various parameters into consideration for the clustering process.

CRITERIA'S CONSIDERED FOR COMPARATIVE STUDY OF CLUSTERING PROTOCOLS

In this chapter, various criteria's considered for the comparison of various forms of clustering protocols are summarized, based on the usage, functionalities and process valuation based comparison criteria's are used. The criteria's considered for the various forms of clustering protocols for the evaluation of performance of various different clustering protocols are lifetime, delay, stability, energy consumption and processing complexity, and the simulation results are discussed. These criteria's gives the various results obtained by the clustering protocols, which gives the overall view of protocols performance (Donta et al , 2020a; Rawat and chauhan 2021c).

Type of network

In 2018 Rostami et al . developed that the clustering approach can be followed based on either homogeneous or heterogeneous type of networks. In the first type, homogeneous, all the nodes present in the WSN are provided with similar properties like memory, energy and bandwidth etc.

In the second type, heterogeneous, the nodes of the WSN are enabled with dissimilar properties, where the initial energy level, assigned to each node will be different.

Delay

This parameter can be described as the time required to transmit the data from one particular node of WSN to its BS, basically called as rounds. The transferring process of each node is calculated based on the rounds of clustering protocols. The delay is measured based on the number of rounds handled per unit of time.

Delay = no. Of rounds / time (1)

Energy usage

The energy consumed by each and every nodes of the network is measured in terms of energy consumed for data collection, data transferring and CH selection, cluster formation etc.The energy consumed for transmission of data from each node to its CH and from CH to its BS is referred as energy consumption or usage. The clustering protocols are constructed in such a way to reduce the energy consumption of each and every node to increase the overall performance of WSN. The average energy consumed by the nodes is measured as:

$$E_{avg} = [\ \Sigma^{n\ to}{}_{i=1}\ E_l\ ]\ /\ n \quad (2)$$

$E_{avg,}$ the average energy, E_l , the level of energy of each node, n is the node representation.

Survival time: The survival time of the network is considered as one of the major parameter in calculating the performance of network. It can be measured based on total number of round to the last node death. The clustering protocol proves the increase in survival time of WSN at a rapid pace. The important objective of clustering protocol is increasing the survival time of the network.

Survival time = total no. Of rounds

-------------------------- (3)

Presence of last node in WSN

Stability: Stability is one of major criteria in measuring the performance of traditional type of clustering protocols. It can be calculated on the basis of time to the number of rounds from beginning of the network to the exit of first node from the network. The clustering protocols gives the increase in performance in terms of stability of the node in cluster based WSN.

Stability = total no. Of rounds

-------------------------------- (4)

Exit of first node

Processing Complexity: It's a normal guess that processing of data in a WSN seems to be very complex, because it consist of a number of process to execute at a random time, the various process like computation of algorithms, memory consumed for data aggregation & communication & the time consumed for running different modules of the protocols. The clustering protocol with various difference parameters will lead to increase the complexity nature of the WSN.

CONCLUSION

Clustering protocol plays an major role in the study of WSN, its potential proves that the lifetime of WSN immensely increased. In this chapter We focused on different clustering protocols and its parameter, classification & comparison based on various parameter influenced by cluster such as increasing network survival time, energy usage, scalability, throughput, coverage, Load balancing. We also discussed on two major classifications of cluster protocols such as traditional clustering approach and fuzzy-logic-based clustering technique. Finally we summarised on the criteria's considered for comparative study of clustering protocol such as network type, delay, lifetime, energy consumption, stability, processing complexity.

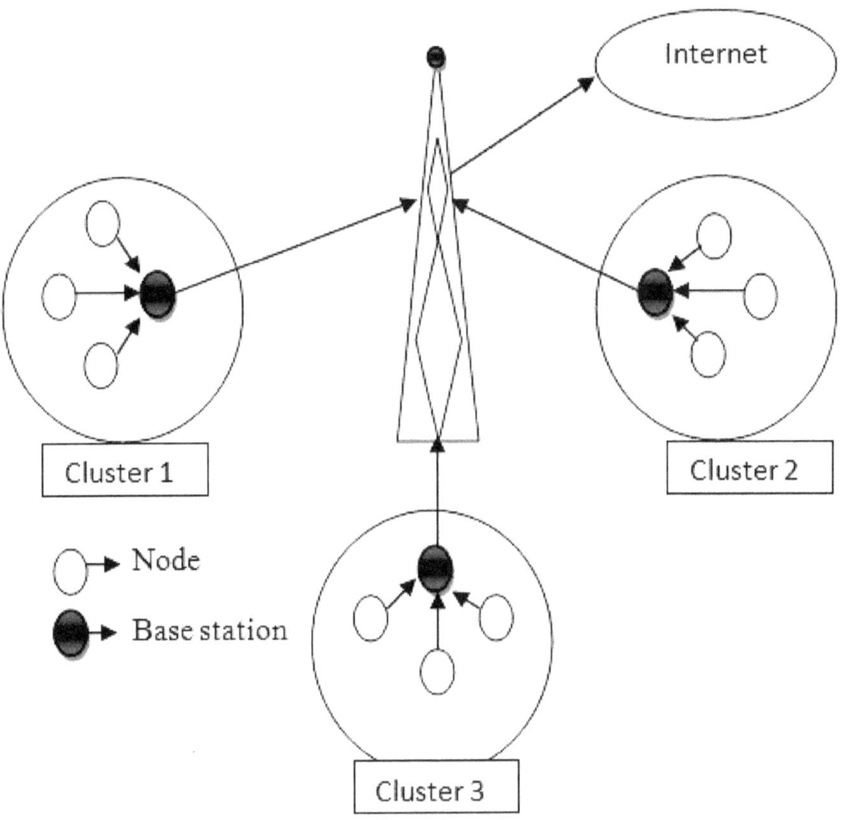

Figure 1 Cluster based WSN

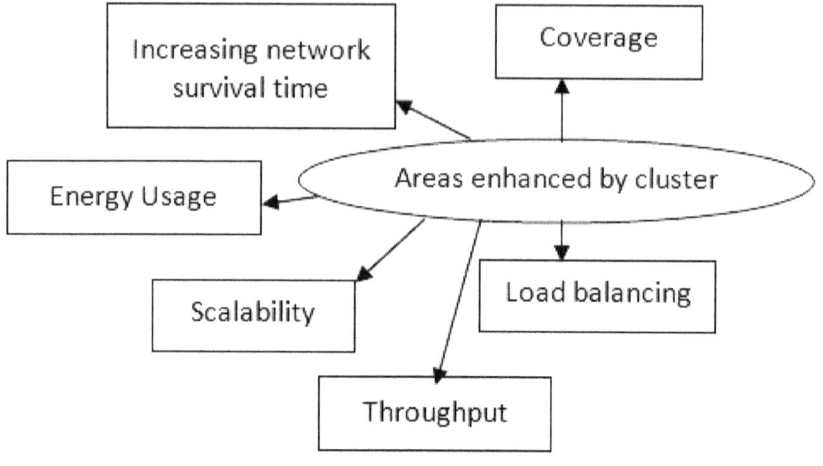

Figure 2. Parameters influenced by clustering

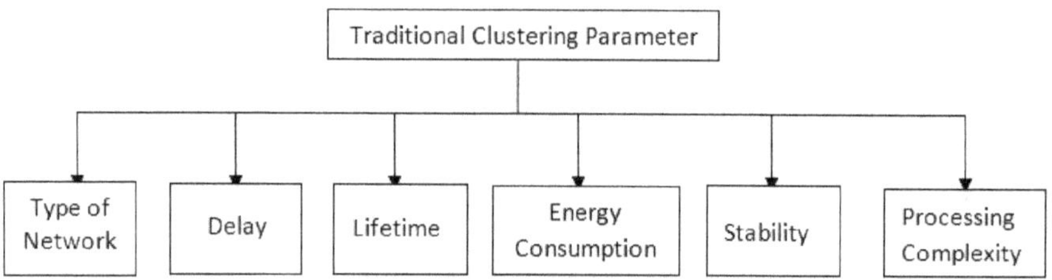

Figure 3. List of Parameter for traditional Clustering Protocols

Table 1: Comparison of clustering techniques

Author	Year	Methodology	Parameter
Al-karki and kamal	2004	Clustering protocol categorization into flat, location-based as hierarchical protocols based on network topology and further classification into QoS-based, negotiation-based, query-based, multipath-based as based on protocol functions	Scalability, Mobility, Energy consumption, Data collection, QoS
Akkaya & Younis	2005	Clustering protocol categorization into data centric, location-based, and hierarchical protocols.	QoS, Network flow
Kumarawadu et al	2008	Clustering protocol based on identity, adjacent node information, biologically inspired and probabilistic	Scalability, Security, QoS, CH selection, Load balancing, Energy usage
Abbasi & Younis	2007	Clustering protocol based on time, constant convergence and variable convergence	Location identity, Cluster overload, stability, Convergence rate, Mobility
Deosarkar et al	2008	Clustering protocol based on deterministic, adaptive, hybrid and combined	CH creation, formation, distribution, re-clustering, selection, balancing
Boyinode et al	2010	Clustering protocol classification into distributed, centralized and hybrid	CH formation & distribution, throughput, size of cluster, hops, energy consumption
Li et al	2011	Clustering protocol based on energy balancing and usage, and control overhead	CH selection, data collection, memory topology, multipath routing
Singh et al 2017	2017	Clustering protocol based on hop as single hop and multi hop	Scalability, Clustering, Load balancing, throughput, Energy usage
Rostami et al	2018	Clustering protocol based on behaviour properties like properties like heterogeneous & homogeneous	Inter-cluster, Intra-cluster communication, throughput, topology, overhead, CH parameter
Sharma et al	2019	Clustering protocol classification into computation, link and energy-based	CH parameter, heterogeneity

Table 2: Evaluation of Performance for Traditional Clustering approach

Protocol	Network type	Delay	Energy usage	Survival time	Stability	Complexity
LEACH (2000)	Homogeneous	Low	High	Low	Low	High
LEACH-M(2006)	Homogeneous	Moderate	High	Low	Low	Moderate
Enhanced-LEACH (2012)	Homogeneous	Moderate	Moderate	Moderate	Moderate	Moderate
IB-LEACH(2014)	Homogeneous	Moderate	Low	High	Moderate	Low
LEACH-MAC(2016)	Homogeneous	Low	Moderate	Moderate	Low	High
TEEN(2001)	Homogeneous	Low	High	Low	Low	High

REFERENCES

[1]Garcia-hernandez CF, Ibargüengoytia-gonzález PH, García-hernández J, Pérez-díaz JA (2007) Wireless sensor networks and applica- tions : a survey. J Comput Sci 7:264–273. https://doi.org/10. 1109/MC.2002.1039518

[2] Ali SM, Sattar A, Shah N, Alam Khan S, Srinivasa Rao D (2019) Wireless sensor networks routing design issues: a survey. Int J Comput Appl 178:975–8887.

[3] Saranya S, Princy M (2012) Routing techniques in sensor network—a survey. In: Procedia engineering. Elsevier Ltd, pp 2739–2747.

[4] Chithaluru P, Tiwari R, Kumar K (2019) AREOR-adaptive ranking based energy efficient opportunistic routing scheme in wireless sensor network. Comput Netw 162:106863. https://doi.org/10. 1016/ j.comnet.2019.106863.

[5] Rawat P, Chauhan S (2021c) Clustering protocols in wireless sensor net- work: a survey, classification, issues, and future directions. Comput Sci Rev 40:100396. https://doi.org/10.1016/j.cosrev.2021.100396.

[6] Liu X (2012) A survey on clustering routing protocols in wireless sen- sor networks. Sensors 12:11113–11153. https://doi.org/10.3390/ s120811113.

[7] Zeb A, Islam AKMM, Zareei M et al (2016) Clustering analysis in wireless sensor networks: the ambit of performance metrics and schemes taxonomy. Int J Distrib Sens Netw 12:4979142. https:// doi.org/10.1177/ 155014774979142.

[8] Al-Karaki JN, Kamal AE (2004) Routing techniques in wireless sensor networks: a survey. IEEE Wirel Commun 11:6–27. https://doi. org/ 10.1109/MWC.2004.1368893.

[9] Akkaya K, Younis M (2005) A survey on routing protocols for wireless sensor networks. Ad Hoc Netw 3:325–349. https://doi.org/10. 1016/j.adhoc.2003.09.010

[10] Abbasi AA, Younis M (2007) A survey on clustering algorithms for wireless sensor networks. Comput Commun 30:2826–2841. https://doi.org/10.1016/j.comcom.2007.05.024

[11] Kumarawadu P, Dechene DJ, Luccini M, Sauer A (2008) Algorithms for node clustering in wireless sensor networks: a survey. In: Proceedings of the 2008 4th international conference on informa- tion and automation for sustainability, ICIAFS 2008, pp 295–300.

[12] Deosarkar BP, Yadav NS, Yadav RP (2008) Clusterhead selection in clustering algorithms for wireless sensor networks: A survey. In: Proceedings of the 2008 international conference on computing, communication and networking, ICCCN 2008.

[13] Boyinbode O, Le H, Mbogho A et al (2010) A survey on clustering algorithms for wireless sensor networks. In: Proceedings— 13th

international conference on network-based information systems, NBiS 2010, pp 358–364.

[14] Li C, Zhang H, Hao B, Li J (2011) A survey on routing protocols for large-scale wireless sensor networks. Sensors 11:3498–3526. https://doi.org/10.3390/s110403498.

[15] Singh AK, Purohit N (2014) An optimised fuzzy clustering for wireless sensor networks. Int J Electron 101:1027–1041. https://doi.org/ 10.1080/00207217.2013.805387.

[16] Rostami AS, Badkoobe M, Mohanna F et al (2018) Survey on cluster- ing in heterogeneous and homogeneous wireless sensor networks. Springer, New York.

[17] Sharma D, Ojha A, Bhondekar AP (2019) Heterogeneity considera- tion in wireless sensor networks routing algorithms: a review. Springer, New York.

[18] Gherbi C, Aliouat Z, Benmohammed M (2017) A survey on cluster- ing routing protocols in wireless sensor networks. Sens Rev 37:12–25.

[19] Priyadarshi R, Rawat P, Nath V (2018a) Energy dependent cluster formation in heterogeneous wireless sensor network. Microsyst Technol. https://doi.org/10.1007/s00542-018-4116-7.

[20] Rawat P, Chauhan S (2020) Probability based cluster routing protocol for wireless sensor network. J Ambient Intell Humaniz Comput 1:3. https://doi.org/10.1007/s12652-020-02307-1.

[21] Sharma S, Jena SK (2015) Cluster based multipath routing protocol for wireless sensor networks. In: Computer communication review. association for computing machinery, pp 14–20.

[22] Rawat P, Chauhan S (2018b) Energy efficient clustering in heteroge- neous environment. In: 2018 second international conference on inventive communication and computational technologies (ICICCT). IEEE, pp 388–392.

[23] Marappan P, Rodrigues P (2016) An energy efficient routing proto- col for correlated data using CL-LEACH in WSN. Wirel Netw 22:1415–1423. https://doi.org/10.1007/s11276-015-1063-4.

[24] Yuvaraja M, Sabrigiriraj M (2017) Fault detection and recovery scheme for routing and lifetime enhancement in WSN. Wirel Netw 23:267–277. https://doi.org/10.1007/s11276-015-1141-7.

[25] Rajpoot P, Dwivedi P (2020) Optimized and load balanced clustering for wireless sensor networks to increase the lifetime of WSN using MADM approaches. Wirel Netw 26:215–251. https://doi. org/

10.1007/s11276-018-1812-2.

[26] Gupta P, Sharma AK (2019) Designing of energy efficient stable clustering protocols based on BFOA for WSNs. J Ambient Intell Humaniz Comput 10:681–700. https://doi.org/10.1007/ s12652-018-0719-1.

[27] Kumaresan K, Kalyani SN (2020) Energy efficient cluster based multi- level hierarchical routing for multi-hop wireless sensor network. J Ambient Intell Humaniz Comput 1:3. https://doi.org/10.1007/ s12652-020-01700-0.

[28] Das S, Barman S, Sinha JD (2012) Energy efficient routing in wireless sensor network. Procedia Technol 6:731–738. https://doi.org/10. 1016/j.protcy.2012.10.088.

[29] Naranjo PGV, Shojafar M, Mostafaei H et al (2017) P-SEP: a prolong stable election routing algorithm for energy-limited heteroge- neous fog-supported wireless sensor networks. J Supercomput 73:733–755. https://doi.org/10.1007/s11227-016-1785-9.

[30] Shokouhifar M, Jalali A (2015) A new evolutionary based application specific routing protocol for clustered wireless sensor networks. AEU Int J Electron Commun 69:432–441. https://doi.org/10. 1016/ j.aeue.2014.10.023.

[31] Ennajari H, Ben Maissa Y, Mouline S (2017) Energy efficient in-network aggregation algorithms in wireless sensor networks: a survey. Lect Notes Electr Eng 397:135–148. https://doi.org/10. 1007/ 978-981-10-1627-1_11.

[32] Mazumdar N, Om H (2018) Distributed fuzzy approach to unequal clustering and routing algorithm for wireless sensor networks. Int J Commun Syst. https://doi.org/10.1002/dac.3709..

[33] Nehra V, Sharma AK, Tripathi RK (2020) FIEPE: fuzzy inspired energy efficient protocol for heterogeneous wireless sensor net- work. Wirel Pers Commun 110:1769–1794. https://doi.org/10.1007/ s11277-019-06811-2.

[34] Yi D, Yang H (2016) HEER—a delay-aware and energy-efficient routing protocol for wireless sensor networks. Comput Netw104:155–173. https://doi.org/10.1016/J.COMNET.2016.04.022.

[35] Huang CF, Tseng YC (2005) The coverage problem in a wireless sensor network. In: Mobile networks and applications. Springer Science + Business Media, Inc. Manufactured in The Netherlands, pp 519–528.

[36] Sari A, Caglar E (2017) Load balancing algorithms and protocols to enhance quality of service and performance in data of WSN. In: Security

and resilience in intelligent data-centric systems and communication networks. Elsevier, pp 143–178.

[37] Hamzah A, Shurman M, Al-Jarrah O, Taqieddin E (2019) Energy-efficient fuzzy-logic-based clustering technique for hierarchical routing protocols in wireless sensor networks. Sensors (basel). https://doi.org/ 10.3390/s19030561.

[38] Singh AK, Purohit N, Varma S (2013) Fuzzy logic based clustering in wireless sensor networks: a survey. Int J Electron 100:126–141.

[39] Donta PK, Amgoth T, Annavarapu CSR (2020a) An extended ACO-based mobile sink path determination in wireless sensor net- works. J Ambient Intell Humaniz Comput 1:3. https://doi.org/ 10.1007/ s12652-020-02595-7.

[40] Rawat P, Chauhan S (2021c) Clustering protocols in wireless sensor net- work: a survey, classification, issues, and future directions. Comput Sci Rev 40:100396.

https://doi.org/10.1016/j.cosrev.2021.100396.

[41] Chandrakasan A, Balakrishnan H (2000) Energy- efficient communication protocol for wireless microsensor net- works. In: Proceedings of the Hawaii international conference on system sciences. IEEE, p 223.

[42] Qing L, Zhu Q, Wang M (2006) Design of a distributed energy-efficient clustering algorithm for heterogeneous wireless sensor networks. Comput Commun 29:2230–2237. https://doi.org/10.1016/J. COMCOM.2006.02.017.

[43] Attea BA, Khalil EA (2012) A new evolutionary based routing pro- tocol for clustered heterogeneous wireless sensor networks. Appl Soft Comput J 12:1950–1957. https://doi.org/10.1016/j. asoc.2011.04.007

[44] Manjeshwar A, Agrawal DP (2001) TEEN: a routing protocol for enhanced efficiency in wireless sensor networks. In: Proceed- ings 15th international parallel and distributed processing sym- posium. IPDPS 2001. IEEE Computer Society, pp 2009–2015.

[45] Singh SK, Kumar P, Singh JP (2017) A survey on successors of LEACH protocol. IEEE Access 5:4298–4328. https://doi.org/ 10.1109/ ACCESS.2017.2666082

[46] Sharma D, Ojha A, Bhondekar AP (2019) Heterogeneity considera-tion in wireless sensor networks routing algorithms: a review. Springer, New York

CHAPTER FOUR

Fuzzy based clustering (FBC) algorithm for extending the lifetime of WSN

Introduction

Extending the lifetime of the sensor node is one of the major challenging issues for the wireless sensor network. The WSN consists of wireless terminals that involve in monitoring hard cored environment with of different nature and parameter that differs based on the applications implemented. These networks with stable infrastructure is embedded with sensor nodes that used to sense a area of particular range and gather information and deliver it to the moderate controller named as cluster head. Here in this sensor network architecture sensor nodes are packed densely within a cluster and these entire cluster grouped together to form a wireless sensor network. These cluster heads aggregate the information and further move it to the central controller called as Base station or sink. Further analysis, processing of data will be done by sink and the action required will be initiated based on the report generated after analysis process. The energy usage by the sensors in each & every cluster to be managed efficiently in order to increase the survival time of each & every sensor node. To attain this efficient clustering algorithm to be developed which could perform cluster based operations effectively. Here in this chapter we concentrates on designing a fuzzy based clustering algorithm for energy efficient dynamic cluster head (CH) selection. This algorithm focuses on solving the position of ineffective usage of unbalanced energy among the cluster head. The simulation results reveal that the fuzzy based clustering algorithm extends the lifetime of WSN by outperforming the previously defined algorithms.

Terminologies : Fuzzy logic, Clustering, network lifetime, cluster head selection, Base station

OVERVIEW

Nowadays the IOT enabled architecture and environments consist of embedded systems of group of sensors that acts as sensor networks operated using wireless protocols results in IOT enabled wireless sensor networks supports in different applications like healthcare monitoring, surveillance of home automation system. Forest fire, structural monitoring, precision based agriculture, military surveillance, under water ocean monitoring, disaster monitoring, traffic monitoring and wildlife monitoring. Recently researchers are focusing on various major problem areas like energy management in the sensor nodes and routing of data in WSNs.

The work of each and every sensor node in the WSN is to sense the physical object present in the environment and transmit it to the central controller of the network called as sink or Base station.The major problem in the WSN is management of energy among the sensor nodes and energy dissipation problem and consumption of more energy for the transmission process comparing to computation and sensing.

It was found that there was more energy consumption for single bit transmission.Therefore in order to manage this problem using various technological parameters like topology, information aggregation and processing and radio scheduling.

In order to extend the lifetime of WSN two strategies is followed they are routing and clustering.Based on some specific properties, the sensor nodes (SNs) are grouped together into one particular group called cluster. Though there is more number of sensor nodes in a cluster one among the cluster will be selected as cluster head (CH) based on the residual energy within the sensor node. The sensor node with more energy will be elected as CH. The cluster head(CH) will aggregate all the information collected by the sensor node of corresponding cluster and will disseminate the information to the Base station o sink either using a single hop or multi communication.

Hence this chapter we focuses on few of the problems in relation with selection of CH in a clustering technique in order to increase the lifetime of WSN based on Fuzzy logic system and evaluating the various paramters and defining the chances for sensors to act as CH among a clusters. The remaining part of the chapter structured as follows section which covers the literature review, in relation with WSN and discusses the developed FBOCS algorithm, and shows Simulation results of the developed algorithm and gives the conclusion of the chapter.

Two types of architectures are followed in the WSN, that are named as homogeneous and heterogeneous network based on the energy level used by the sensor nodes .In the homogeneous type of WSN, all the sensor nodes posses same amount of energy, at the same time in the heterogeneous type of WSN, only few of the sensor nodes assigned with more amount of initial energy. Comparing to the other entire sensor node in the network, the clustering based WSN is one of the best approach to manage the energy consumption efficiently. The nodes in the WSN are grouped into various sub groups and for each group one particular sensor node will be selected to act as cluster Head (CH) that handle major transmission process. In this heterogeneous type of WSN, each sensor node with different properties and the node with high processing ability, high computing and high energy will be selected as CH. There are two forms of CH, static and dynamic. The static CH will act as a CH until losing all its energy and becomes dead node . The dynamic cluster head (CH) will act as a CH and after losing all its energy, transfer the control to another sensor node that have high level of energy The selection of cluster head is one of the important processes in managing the lifetime of the network . The cluster head receives all the information from the other entire sensor node in a cluster and forward it to the BS or sink.

DATA AGGREGATION

The key problem to be focussed for WSN is controlling of the sensor nodes and consumption of energy. To use the energy consumed by sensor nodes properly, these could be followed such as range of the communication could be shortened, decreasing the total number of transmissions between the sensor nodes and between the sensor nodes and sink.The Comparison of fuzzy based algorithm shown in Table 1.

The clustering based arrangement of sensor nodes gives a better results for reduced energy consumption of SNs in WSN. One of the key issues are election of the cluster head(CH) and its formation of sensor nodes as cluster.There are lots of current protocols that gives the various formulation for both the CH selection and formation of clusters. Here some of the protocols followed the process of fuzzy logic system in choosing the cluster head and cluster formation. This fuzzy logic procedure mainly follows four important steps such as fuzzification, defuzzification, and Fuzzy rule and inference engine .

In 202 Mehra etal developed a algorithm called as FBECS – Fuzzy based enhanced cluster head selection focuses on the residual energy of the node, distance between sensor node and sink, density of the node, and fuzzy system input. The selection of cluster head(CH) is based on chance for each node and HEI(High eligibility index).Here the discussion is related to selection of CH and not describing any optimal solution for cluster formation.

In 2018 Agrawal and pandey developed a FUCA – Fuzzy based unequal clustering algorithm, in this algorithm using fuzzy based system, the CH is selected and various inputs for the system is its density, distance between the sensor node to CH and CH to base station, and residual energy. The output obtained is rank and competition radius. The algorithms do not focus on the rotation of the role of sensor as cluster head.

In 2019 Hamzah et al , introduce an algorithm called as FLEEC/D fizzy logic based energy efficient clustering for WSN focuses on the minimum distance allocation between the CHs various inputs considered for this chapter are node density, location based placement of sensor, residual energy of the node, and distance to the BS from sensor node. The output calculated is the chance for the sensor node to act as CH. In this chapter assignment of same sensor node as cluster head for one or more time, drastically increases the survival time of network.

In 2020 Bayrakdar , discusses on various techniques and simulations for WSN. The concepts like TDMA-Time division multiple access was used for fetching the medium to transmission of data and other techniques like Ricean and Rayleigh fading channels has been used.

There are 5 way of clustering called as spectral, partition-based, grid-based, hierarchical, and density based are given in Table 1.

Fuzzy based clustering algorithm

In this algorithm, various input parameter have been used as an input to the fuzzy system, various inputs are residual energy, density and distance to sink.In this fuzzy based system the residual energy is assigned with three linguistic variables low, medium, high and the distance to sink is allotted with two linguistics variable as Near, Far, and the input variable for density is assigned with three linguistic variable as low, medium, and high shown in Table 1.

The output variable is the chance of election as CH with various linguistic variables like H, M, L, VH, VL, HM, RL, RH.This algorithm is used to select the sensor node as cluster head based on various input variable and these variable get processed by algorithm and finally the better solution is provided in order to choose the best sensor node as CH cluster head.

In this developed algorithm two member function are used one as trapezoidal member function for calculating the residual energy, density and chance and the triangular member function, is used for calculated the distance to the sink,Using the fuzzification mode the input variable are processed using the FBDCS algorithm, and the inference engine was used for inferring, and the results are drawn from the rule consists of various conditions.By using the defuzzification method, the resultant output is obtained.

Algorithm : FBC(Fuzzy based clustering) - Pseudocode

Input : n(number of sensor node), m cluster, residual energy R, Distance to Sink DTS, Density D

Output: election of CH node.

Initialization k = N1,N2...........Nn sensors

C = C1,C2...............Cn cluster

For I = 1 to k

For j = 1 to C

Cahnce[l] = fuzzy(N, C, R, DTS, D)

If C(n) is active

Check each N, R && DTS

If n(R) > = Th(R) && DTS < = Th(DTS)

Choose N as CH

If N has already acted as CH

Compare n with all the other Nn.

Th(R) && DTS

Reassign max 3 times

If D is > = Th(D)

Choose N(min(DTS))

Else

Check each N(R) >= Th (R)

Choose N as CH

End For

End For

CH = max(chance(l)

Introduce the CH as cluster head to all the sensor nodes of the corresponding cluster

SIMULATION PARAMETERS

Table 2: The simulation for the developed FBDCS protocol is done using MATLAB tool, for the simulation process, the total number of nodes used is around 500 deployed in an network area of standard size is (100 X 100) m. Here all the transmission process follows single source to single destination combination, with dynamic multi point model followed to fetch the node locations. The packet size used is 3000 bits for both the data and control packets.

SIMULATION RESULTS

In this chapter, the simulation results are compared with standard existing protocols like FBECS, FLEEC/D and FUCA. There are 500 nodes deployed in the area of 100m X 100m and BS is approximated at the location of 50m X 50m.The architecture followed over here for the deploment of sensor node is homogeneous that is all the sensor nodes has similar memory, process, and initial energy.Two parameter were focussed to shows the results of the algorithm, one is lifetime of WSN and the other one is the residual energy of the network calculated based on remaining energy level of all the n sensor present in the network.

1.Lifetime

By comparing with the standard existing algorithm, such as FBECS,FLEEC/D, and FUCA the results were obtained.The lifetime of the sensor network is calculated based on number of alive nodes after certain number of rounds, Rounds of the WSN is calculated based on the number of transmission achieved in particuar time. By simulating this algorithm and while comparing it with other, it gives efficient performance in terms of total number of alive nodes after n rounds.

2. *Residual energy*

The residual energy is measured based on the consolidation of remaining energy level of all the sensors in the WSN after completing each round.The parameter like(AEDR) – average energy dissipation per round is measured.The ratio for the residual energy is calculated based on the average energy of all the sensor nodes to the number of alive sensor nodes.In this developed algorithm the residual energy level obtained by comparing with the existing protocol like FLEEC/D, FBEV, and the FBOCS shows high value for the residual energy as 20%, 42%, 68%.

The developed algorithm results on the better performance by comparing with the existing protocols due to efficient formation and cluster head selected using the fuzzy based algorithm.

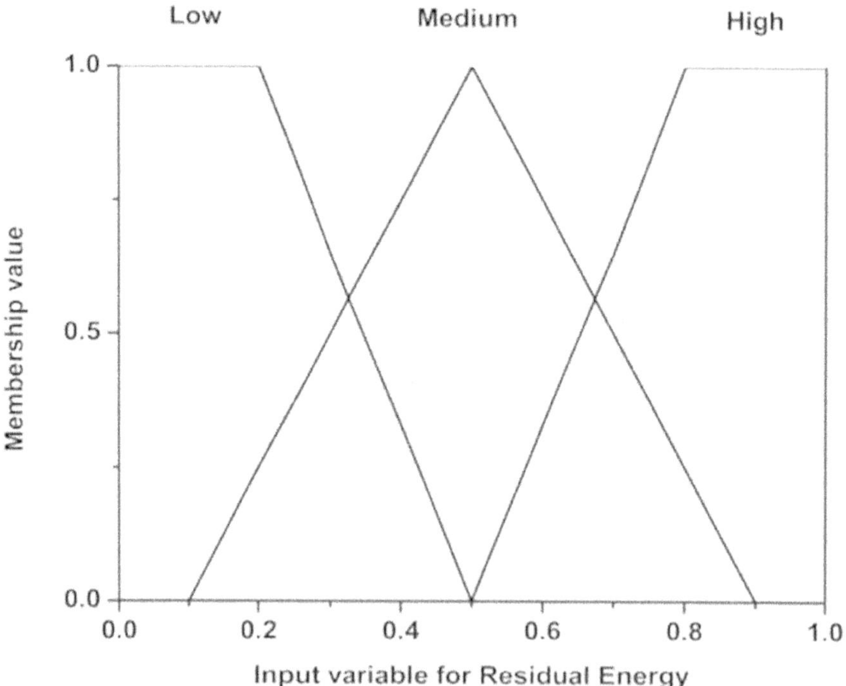

Figure 1: Residual Energy Linguistic variable

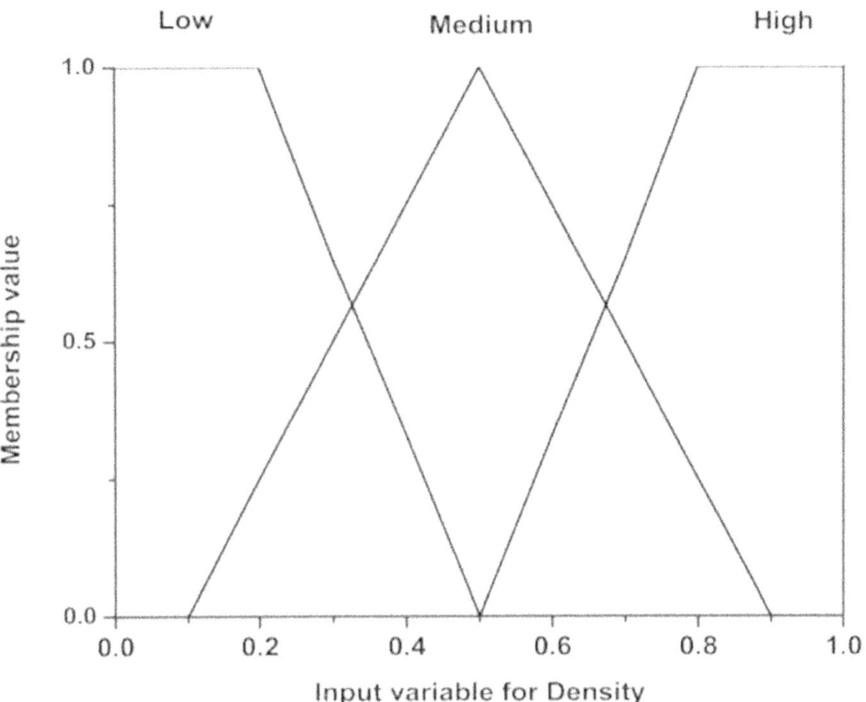

Figure 2: Density Linguistic variable

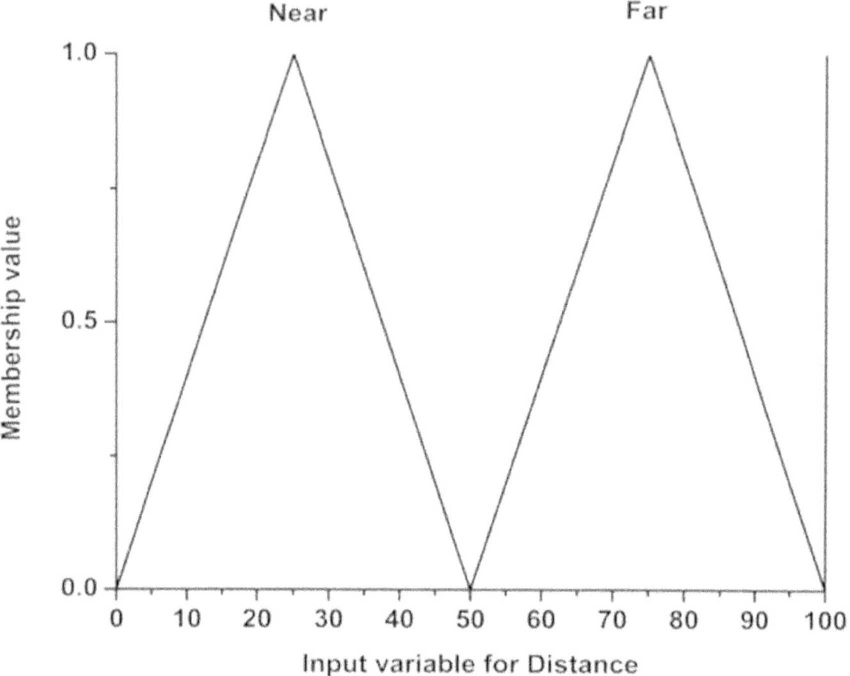

Figure 3: Distance Linguistic variable

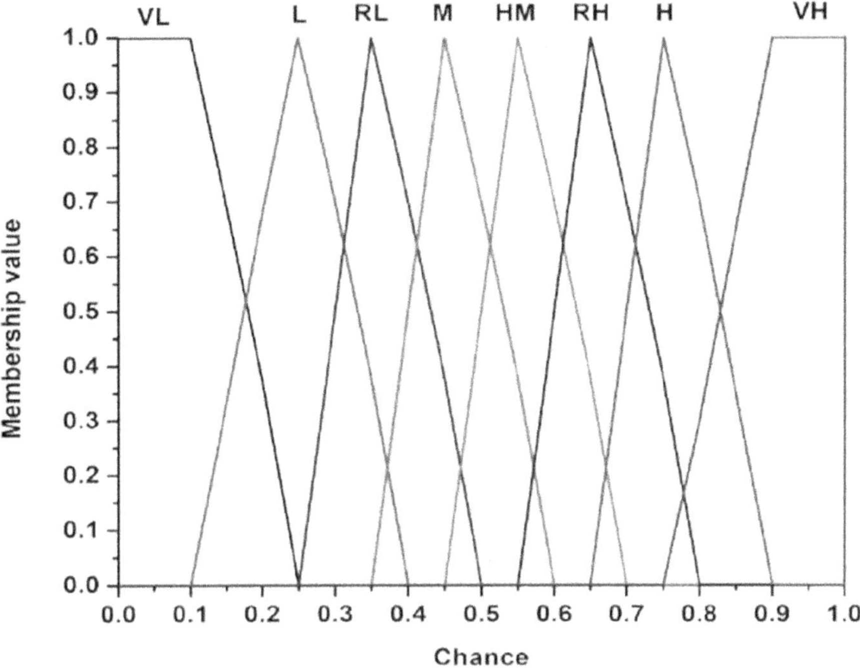

Figure 4: Output chance Linguistic variable

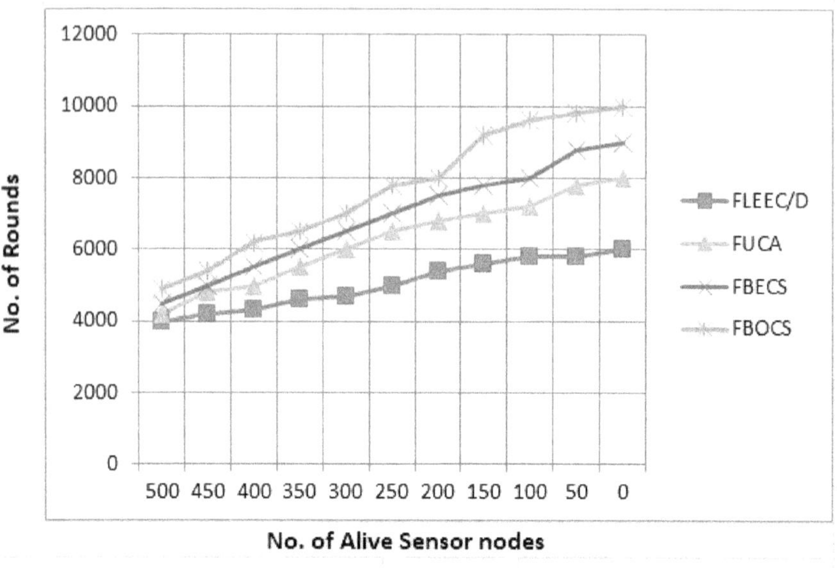

Figure 5: Lifetimeof WSN

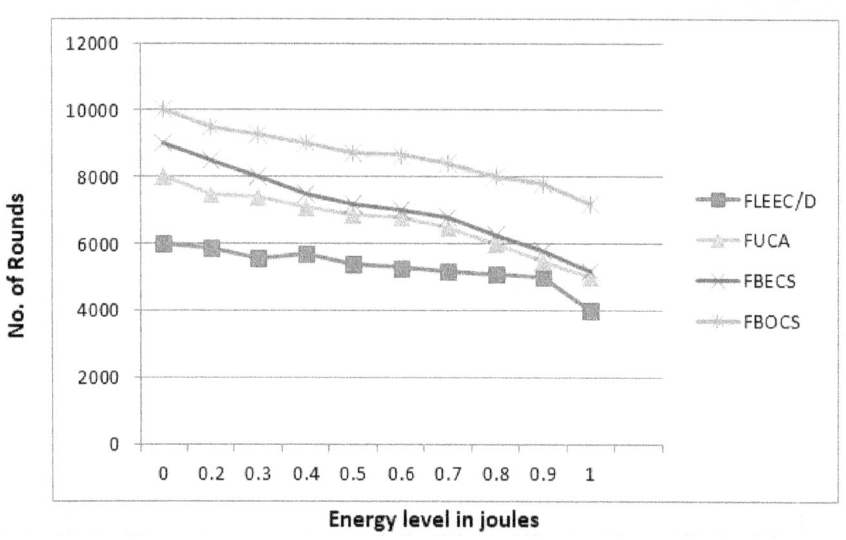

Figure 6: Residual energy of WSN

S. No.	DTS	R	D	chance
1	Near	Very High	High	Very high
2	Far	Very High	High	Very high
3	Near	Very High	Medium	Very high
4	Far	Very High	Medium	Very high
5	Near	Very High	Low	High
6	Far	Very High	Low	High
7	Near	High	High	Very high
8	Far	High	High	High
9	Near	High	Medium	Very high
10	Far	High	Medium	High
11	Near	High	Low	High Medium
12	Far	High	Low	Rather High
13	Near	Medium	High	Very high
14	Far	Medium	High	High
15	Near	Medium	Medium	High Medium
16	Far	Medium	Medium	Medium
17	Near	Medium	Low	Rather Low
18	Far	Medium	Low	Low
19	Near	Low	High	High Medium
20	Far	Low	High	Rather High
21	Near	Low	Medium	Medium
22	Far	Low	Medium	Low
23	Near	Low	Low	Low
24	Far	Low	Low	Very Low

Table 1: Fuzzy Variables

Parameter	Values
Area	100 m X 100 m
Simulation software	MATLAB
Initial energy of the node	2 J
Data packet size	3000 b
Ee(Et & Er)	50nJ/bit
Th(d)	5m
Number of sensors	500
Th(DTS)	3m

Table 2: Simulation Parameters

CONCLUSION

The management of sensor nodes in terms of lifetime and energy seems to be the major challenges in the WSN. The fuzzy based system provides a better solution to reduce the energy usage and maintain the residual energy below the threshold level which help to increase the survival time of the network.The developed FBOCS algorithm which outperformed while comparing with the other standard algorithm like FLEEC/D, FBECS, and FUCA.

REFERENCES

[1] R.S. Sudha, A survey on wireless sensor networks, Int. J. Eng. Sci. Res. Technol. (2017) 66–71.

[2] K.K. Kaur, Parneet, S. Singh, Wireless sensor network: architecture, design issues and applications, Int. J. Sci. Eng. Res. (IJSER) (2014) 6–10.

[3] S.R. Prasanna, Srinivasa, An overview of wireless sensor networks applications and security, Int. J. Soft Comput. Eng. (IJSCE) (2012) 538–540.

[4] A.K. Priyanka, Singh, A survey on applications, communication stack and energy consumptions in WSNs, Int. J. Recent Technol. Eng. (IJRTE) (2019).

[5] T.B. Bala, Varsha, S. Kumawat, V. Jaglan, A survey: issues and challenges in wireless sensor network, Int. J. Eng. Technol. (2018) 53–55.

[6] M.A.I. Matin, Wireless Sensor Networks Technology and Protocols, M M, Intechopen, 2012.

[7] S.K.S. Gupta, Poonam, Overview of wireless sensor network: a survey, Int. J. Adv. Res. Comput. Commun. Eng. (2014) 5201–5207.

[8] P.R.C. Gundalwar, A literature review on Wireless Sensor Networks (WSNs) and its diversified applications, Int. J. Adv. Res. Comput. Sci. (2012) 120–128.

[9] L S.F. Chelouah, L. Bouallouche-Medjkoune, Localization protocols for mobile wireless sensor networks: a survey, Comput. Electr. Eng. (2017) 1–19.

[10] C.Y.-C. Wu, Heterogeneous wireless sensor network deployment and topology control based on irregular sensor model, in: Second International Conference on Grid and Pervasive Computing, Paris, France, 2007.

[11] R.H. Sankar, S. Venkatasubramanian, A study on next generations heterogeneous sensor networks, in: 5th IEEE GCC Conference & Exhibition, Kuwait, 2009.

[12] A. Sharma, Study of different network topologies, Int. J. Res. Publ. Semin. (JRPS) (2016).

[13] K.H.B. Krishna, Y. Suresh, T. Kumar, Wireless sensor network topology control using clustering, in: 7th International Conference on Communication, Computing and Virtualization 2016, 2016, pp. 893–902.

[14] A.V.P. Nagpure, Sulabha, Topology control in wireless sensor network: an overview, Int. J. Comput. Appl. (IJCA) (2014) 13–18.

[15] V. Ramasamy, Mobile wireless sensor networks: an overview. Wireless Sensor Networks - Insights and Innovations, IntechOpen, 2017.

[16] T B.J. Camp, V. Davies, A survey of mobility models for ad hoc network research, Wireless Commun. Mob. Comput. 2 (2002).

[17] V R.K.M. Vasanthi, A. Ajith Singh, M. Hemalatha, A detailed study of mobility models in wireless, J. Theor. Appl. Inf. Technol. 33 (2011) 7–14.

[18] R Z.Z. Silva, J.S. Silva, V. Vassiliou, Mobility in WSNs for critical applications, in: IEEE Symposium on Computers and Communications (ISCC '11), Corfu. Greece, 2011, pp. 451–456.

[19] R. RR, Handbook of Mobile Ad Hoc Networks for Mobility Models, Springer, 2011.

[20] N.B. Malik, Anju, Literature review on protocols for wireless sensor networks, J. Netw. Commun. Emerg. Technol. (JNCET) (2017) 17–22.

[21] K.P. Mehta, Raju, Energy efficient routing protocols for wireless sensor networks: a survey, Int. J. Comput. Appl. (IJCA) (2017) 41–46.

[22] L.K.Z. Ketshabetswe, A. Murtala, M. Mangwala, J.M. Chuma, B. Sigweni, Communication protocols for wireless sensor networks: a survey and comparison, Heliyon (2019) pp. 1-43.

[23] V.C. R.P. Biradar, S.R. Sawant, R.R. Mudholkar, Classification and comparison of routing protocols in wireless sensor networks Ubiquitous Comput. Secur. Syst. J. (UbiCC) (2010) 704–711.

[24] S.G. Kaganurmath, Evaluation of routing protocols for wireless sensor networks, Int. J. Comput. Commun. Technol. (2016).

[25] M.D. Radi, Behnam, K.A. Bakar, M. Lee, Multipath routing in wireless sensor networks: survey and research challenges, Sensors (2012) 650–685.

[26] A.M. Sarkar, Senthil, Routing protocols for wireless sensor networks: what the literature says? Alex. Eng. J. (2016) 3173–3183.

[27] S.S.H. Arathi, Flat based network routing protocol in wireless sensor network, Int.J. Eng. Res. Technol. (IJERT) (2015).

[28] C.D. Choksi, Bijon, Comparison of routing protocols in wireless sensor networks, in: International Conference on Computer Science and Information Technology, 2012, pp. 17–23.

[29] C.G. Intanagonwiwat, Ramesh, D. Estrin, Directed diffusion: a scalable and robust communication paradigm for sensor networks, in: 6th Annual International Conference on Mobile Computing and Networking, 2002, pp. 56–67.

[30] H.B. Echoukairi, Khalid, M. Ouzzif, A survey on flat routing protocols in wireless sensor networks, in: International Symposium on Ubiquitous Networking, 2016, pp. 311–324.

[31] S. Giordano, I. Stojmenovic, L. Blazevic, Position based routing algorithms for ad hoc networks: a taxonomy, Ad hoc Wirel. Netw. (2003).

[32] I. Stojmenovic, Position-based routing in ad hoc networks, IEEE Commun. Mag. (2002) 128–134.

[33] Y. Yu, R. Govindan, D. Estrin, Geographical and Energy Aware Routing: A Recursive Data Dissemination Protocol for Wireless Sensor Networks, UCLA Computer Science Department, 2001.

[34] F. Kuhn, R. Wattenhofer, A. Zollinger, Asymptotically optimal geometric mobile ad-hoc routing, in: 6th international workshop on Discrete algorithms and methods for mobile computing and communications, 2002, pp. 24–33.

[35] J.N.K. Al-Karaki, E. Ahmed, Routing techniques in wireless sensor networks: a survey, Wirel. Commun., IEEE (2005).

[36] C L.M. Arboleda, N. Nasser, Cluster-based routing protocol for mobile sensor networks, in: 3rd international conference on Quality of service in heterogeneous wired/wireless networks, 2006.

[37] J. Hong, J. Kook, S. Lee, et al., T-LEACH: the method of threshold-based cluster head replacement for wireless sensor networks, Inf. Syst. Front. (2009).

[38] R.S.V. Sreejith, N. Vyas, K.R. Anupama, L.J. Gudino, Area based routing protocol for mobile wireless sensor networks, in: 32nd International Conference on Information Networking (ICOIN), 2018.

[39] Reham almesaeed, Ahmed Jedidi , Dynamic directional routing for mobile wireless sensor networks, in : Ad Hoc Networks, Elsevier 2020.

Terminologies

SNs - Sensor nodes

CH - Cluster head

WSN - Wireless sensor network

MAC - Medium access control

LEACH - Low energy adaptive clustering hierarchy

BS - Base station

FBC - Fuzzy based clustering

www.ingramcontent.com/pod-product-compliance
Lightning Source LLC
Chambersburg PA
CBHW052224150726
48002CB00003B/1260